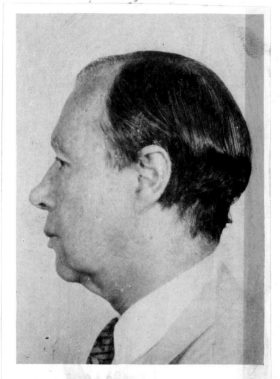

Anthony Rhodes was born in 1916. He
was educated at Rugby, the Royal
Military Academy and Trinity College,
Cambridge. In his first book, the
best-selling *Sword of Bone*, he described
life in the BEF in 1939-40 and the
evacuation of Dunkirk in which he took
part. Invalided from the Army in 1945,
he then taught at Geneva University and
Eton College until 1953, when he became
a full-time writer. He has published
fourteen books—fiction, travel,
biography—the most recent being *The
Vatican in the Age of the Dictators
1922–1945.*

PRINCES OF THE GRAPE

By the same author:

PRINCES
OF THE GRAPE

GREAT WINE MAKERS THROUGH THE AGES

ANTHONY RHODES

WEIDENFELD AND NICOLSON
LONDON

© Anthony Rhodes 1975

Weidenfeld and Nicolson
11 St John's Hill London SW11

ISBN 0 297 76927 8

Printed in Great Britain by
Willmer Brothers Limited, Birkenhead

To

PATRICK FORBES

author of

Champagne, the Wine, the Land, the People

Contents

Illustrations

A*

Preface

The term "Prince of the Grape" was first used by Louis XV to describe the Marquis de Ségur. When that nobleman came to Court the monarch, aware that his subject was richer than himself, said, "*C'est mon Prince de la Vigne.*" The name was apt, for in the mid-eighteenth century the Marquis de Ségur owned three of the finest vineyards in the world, Lafite, Mouton and Latour, and his annual income of £500,000 came principally from the grape. The royal soubriquet remained, and he was thereafter known by it throughout the realm. Much the same could be said for two other eighteenth-century noblemen, the Marquis d'Aulède who owned the equally majestic growths of Margaux and Haut-Brion, and the Marquis de Brassier who owned fabled Beychevelle. After them came a host of other vineyard owners with resounding names – the Marquis de la Tour du Pin, the Marquis de Pontac, the Marquis de Fumel, most famous of all the Baron de la Brède, otherwise known as Montesquieu, who wrote, "What makes me like living at La Brède, is that I feel my money is beneath my feet."

In the eighteenth century these noblemen dominated the wine production of France. They were not ashamed to sell their wine for profit, because this was the one form of commerce which was dignified enough for an aristocrat to engage in. Neither before nor after the eighteenth century did the term "Prince of the Grape" apply so aptly as it did to these great Bordeaux vineyard owners. It was during their beneficent if arbitrary rule that the *grands crus* came to be known as such. Before them, the smaller owners did not possess the means, financial and technical, for producing great wine. The names Lafite, Latour, Margaux, Mouton had not acquired the prestige these eighteenth-century aristocrats gave them, and which they still possess today.

After the departure of these owners at the Revolution, either on the scaffold or by emigration, their properties were sequestrated and sold by auction. The great vineyards passed into profane hands, sometimes one vineyard being parcelled out among fifty small proprietors. Then came the nineteenth century, when the new rich middle classes, the bankers and commercial magnates from Paris, bought up the vineyards. If some of them had the means to emulate their eighteenth-century predecessors and live *en prince* they could no longer, owing to the egalitarian nature of the times, rule over their vineyards *en prince*.

In our own times, the term "Prince" in connection with the grape has taken on an allegorical flavour; for most of the names which dominate the wine trade today do not sound particularly princely – Clicquot, Gilbey, Moët, Martell, Johnston, Taylor, Krug. Yet one of the features of the European wine families is their tendency, whatever their origin, to gravitate towards the aristocracy, generally through marriage. Moët has been directed for over a generation by the de Vogüés, who married into it. The Polignacs control Pommery in much the same way. The bourgeois descendants of the Champagne widow Clicquot married into three of the oldest Dukedoms of France. All the sherry firms are headed by Dukes and Marquises. The Ferreiras of Oporto married into the Royal House of Portugal. The Princes von Metternich who own Johannisberg on the Rhine, are allowed to quarter the Habsburg arms on their escutcheon, as do the Domecqs in Spain.

In the course of many European wanderings since the Second World War, I have been fortunate enough to meet a number of these families. Not only did they invite me into their cellars, but they told me a good deal about the history of their firms, many of which are several centuries old. I have here attempted to describe some of them, in a selection which is bound to be arbitrary. A study of family firms ranging over most of the wine-producing countries of western Europe – which must possess at least a thousand vintners – cannot be comprehensive. My broad aim has been to take one or two representative figures from each country, and to describe them in as much detail as is available. It will be noted that as we retreat in time, this detail becomes less distinct with each receding century. This is primarily due to the lack of archival material about wine personalities in the Classical, Dark and Middle Ages; but also because wine-making was then not as important, nor as technically developed, as it has become in the last two or three centuries.

It will also be noted that all the vintners examined here – from Horace and Ausonius in Classical times, through the Middle Ages with its monkish epicures seated at their refectory tables washing down a haunch of venison with good red Burgundy, until our own times with Philippe de Rothschild extracting his nectar at Mouton – have one thing in common. They all possess that civilised amiability which appears to come from continuous contact with the grape. They are all men of generosity, hospitality and frequently taste. They are not above adulterating their wine if they get the chance, and one or two have done a spell behind bars. But I have never heard any of them described as boorish or elegiac companions. On the contrary down the centuries, in good times as in bad, these men have rejoiced their fellow creatures.

I

Dom Pérignon and his Progeny

In the year 1670, outside the town of Epernay, on the sunny slopes rising from the poplar-fringed Marne, stood in all its glory the royal abbey of St Peters Hautvillers. Its foundation was hallowed by saintly legend. Tradition relates that in the middle of the seventh century its site was dedicated to St Nivard, Bishop of Rheims, by the same snow-white dove which had brought down the Holy Oil for the coronation of Clovis in Rheims. The bird alighted on a tree, and at this exact spot some decades later arose the high altar at which St Berchier was solemnly invested with the symbols of episcopal dignity. Such was the origin of what is today the first shrine to viticulture in the world.

In the Dark and Middle Ages, the great vineyard owners were the abbeys or monasteries. The most important man in city or province was the bishop who incarnated all local authority. One of his functions, at a time when no such thing as a caravanserai existed, was to entertain visiting dignitaries. Wine was an essential part of the fare they were offered; indeed it was a part of mediaeval lore that to fail to serve it to guests was to *manquer d'honneur*. It therefore became the practice in Christian Europe for every bishopric and monastery to possess its own vineyards, the quality of whose wine it could control.

In the late seventeenth century, the vineyards of St Peters Hautvillers were administered by a Benedictine monk, Dom Pérignon – a name destined to gain for the Abbey a fame greater than that of the devoutest of its bishops. Born into the legal bourgeoisie of Rheims, Pierre Pérignon entered the monastery in 1670, and quickly revealed a remarkable palate for tasting and adjudging grapes. "He was unique", wrote a contemporary, "in that he possessed a delicacy of taste so singular that right into extreme old age he could tell precisely from which vineyard a grape came." As well as superintending the Abbey vineyard and the wine-making, his task was to ensure that the tithes, in wine or grapes, were paid by the peasants to their seigniorial lord, the bishop. The produce that came before him was necessarily of different qualities – from which he observed that one kind of soil imparted fragrance to the wine, another generosity, another body, and so forth. He therefore conceived the idea of blending the best wines from the various vineyards – something that had not been thought of before. He also introduced the bark of the cork-tree as a stopper, in place of the tow soaked in oil which had always been used, thereby making it possible to retain the effervescence for much longer. His discovery depended on the fundamental property of the white wine of Champagne to conserve a large part of its natural sugar if properly bottled, and to become sparkling and effervescent in the spring when the sap awakens in the vines.* He regulated the tendency of the local still wine to effervesce by bottling it at a special season of the year, in this way producing a sparkling wine which keeps and which, when poured, overflows the glass.

It was appropriate at this moment in the late seventeenth century when French civilisation was at its height that the discovery should have been made. It seems that Nature deliberately invented this sparkling beverage to revive the spirits of the most civilised court in Europe, after the military reverses which France had received at the hands of Marlborough. The great architects of modern France, Colbert, Louvois and Luxembourg were dead; the Treaty of Ryswick had been signed; the powers of the Sun King were at last on the decline. At this moment of decadence, the men who were to become the future *roués* of the Regency were

*Patrick Forbes, author of the definitive work, *Champagne, the Wine, the Land, the People* writes "It must be remembered that natural effervesence in wine is by no means restricted to the Champagne district. But it manifests itself more powerfully here than anywhere else in the world because of the northern climate where the cold of the winter follows quickly on the gathering of the grapes; and because of certain properties imparted to the wine by the chalky soil of Champagne."

youthful and gay, and the new wine suited their world of laughter, wit and insouciance.

The name which will always be associated with the new sparkling wine is that of Sillery, a family of Rheims. If a simple monk could invent it, it required this brilliant family to make the wine known to the aristocracy of France, and later of Europe. In this sense, Sillery may well be described as the first modern wine firm. In 1543, Pierre Brulart, a bourgeois prominent in the municipal life of Rheims, married an heiress of the Sillery estate who owned some vineyards south-east of Rheims. They were hardly exploited until his grandson became their owner, and immediately realised their possibilities for producing the new sparkling wine. He opened up markets for it in Paris and Belgium, and was soon selling it at the court of France, where he established himself in French society. The most famous member of the Sillerys was his son, Nicolas, who negotiated the Peace of Vervins between France and Spain, for which he was created Marquis de Sillery. He became, successively, Keeper of the Seals, Chancellor of Navarre and Chancellor of France. For the next hundred years, there was seldom a decade in which some high office of state, a governorship or an embassy abroad was not held by a Sillery. And all this came originally from champagne.

Curiously, the fame of this wine was greatly enhanced by the near bankruptcy of the Marquis de Sillery in 1707. As a result of gambling and high living, he had lost his fortune; all that remained to him was the ancestral vineyard outside Epernay. A gourmet, a generous and warm-hearted man, one of the most popular figures at court in the last days of Louis XIV, he took a calculated risk. He gave a magnificent dinner at Versailles, to which he invited all the figures of society who were wine connoisseurs – the Duc de Vendôme, the Marquis d'Estrées, the Marquis de Laval, the Marquis de Chaulieu. At a given signal when the company was gay and garrulous, a dozen buxom damsels draped in the guise of Bacchanals entered the room bearing what appeared at first sight to be baskets of flowers – but which, on being placed before each guest, proved to be flower-enwreathed bottles of the new champagne.

3

At Versailles, this famous dinner was talked about for years, and of the effervescent Sillery wine which "kept you young" and enabled you to sit up all night. Those who had never drunk it before ordered it for their châteaux, and the fortunes of the Marquis de Sillery were restored. He later paid tribute to it in somewhat indifferent verse about that convivial society:

> *Ta mousse, se posant aux lèvres des Marquises*
> *A leur poudre argentée a mêlé ton argent.*
> *Tu es le conseiller d'aventures exquises,*
> *Champagne, et je palpite encore en y songeant.**

Champagne soon flowed in the brilliant circle of periwigged beaux and patched and powdered beauties who formed the court of the Regent, Philippe d'Orléans. Of him, his mother Charlotte of Bavaria wrote, "When Philippe gets drunk, it is not on strong drink and spiritous liqueurs, but on the sparkling wine of Champagne." This is confirmed by the Duc de Saint-Simon who wrote in his memoirs that the Regent seldom went to bed sober, adding, "He drinks too much champagne to be becoming in a Regent of France."

The Regent's notorious *petit soupers* at the Palais Royal were distinguished by the quantities of champagne consumed. Every evening he, his *rouést* and their mistresses would repair to the Palais Royal to sup, drink and gamble. The company included not only aristocrats like the Duchesse de Gesvres, who could drink as well as any man, but pretty girls from the Opera and the play-houses, and clever actors known for their witty tongue and debauched habits. When the doors of the Palais were closed on the company at nine o'clock, birth counted for little, wit for everything. From that moment, there were neither princes nor actors, duchesses nor ballet-girls, neither etiquette nor ceremony; differences of rank were blended in perfect equality and, as Saint-

---

*"Champagne – with the powdered silver on the lips of Marchionesses you mix your silvered foam! Champagne – instigator of the most exquisite intrigues, at whose very thought we thrill again."

†The term was coined jocularly by the Regent for his fellow debauchees. They were such sinners, he mocked, that they deserved to "be broken on the wheel" (*la roue*).

Simon wrote, "The person who could say the most piquant things ruled. Paris might have been in flames, for there was no longer any Regent; he was inaccessible to all his Ministers."

Bottles of the sparkling wine stood in rows on the side-tables, and the Regent himself often tried his hand at cooking some particularly *recherché* dish, while other guests performed the office of waiters. As the evening wore on, the character of everyone at court was passed in review and freely discussed, the gallantries past and present, raking up all the old stories, disputes, jokes, scandals. The company drank into the small hours, the Regent and his favourite daughter, the Duchesse de Berry, setting the example. It was said in Paris that she was his mistress, and that here too they set the fashion in incest.* Sometimes the candles were extinguished and the orgies continued in the dark. On one occasion in the dark the Regent, who was a great practical joker, suddenly threw open wide a cupboard full of blazing candles, and the amorous pairs were caught with their breeches down and skirts up. One of the amusements was for the girls to lie on their backs and be pulled round the room by their legs. Another was the *tableau vivant*, in one of which the Duchesse de Berry with the Duchess de Parabère and the Marquis d'Averne, all stark naked, represented *The Judgement of Paris*, taken most faithfully from the ancient bas-reliefs. Saint-Simon says that prominent among the guests was often the Jesuit priest, Père Rigolet, who "drank enough champagne to make a musketeer stagger, while relating anecdotes which would have brought a blush to the cheeks of the Garde-Française." The Duchesse de Berry always went to bed drunk. It was due to her over-indulgence in champagne at the fatal supper with her father at Meudon in 1722 that she died a week later.

If the new wine unloosed the tongues and breeches of the *roués* at the Palais Royal, and lent sparkle to the eyes of their paramours, it also fired the sallies of the wits and versifiers whom the Duchesse de Maine gathered round her at Sceaux; and it was an

---

*Voltaire's play *Oedipe* contains a number of references to the incestuous relationship between the Regent and his daughter; and La Grange-Chancel devotes the third Ode of his *Philippiques* to it. She possessed three establishments, the Luxembourg where her father visited her daily, Meudon and La Muette. She had 800 servants.

inspiration to the cabaret-haunting poets of that licentious period. It was equally popular with the Regent's successor, Louis xv, enlivening the royal repasts at La Muette, Marly and Choissy. When in 1741 that "well-beloved" king passed through Rheims a local priest, Dom Châtelain, wrote, "It was no longer a question of which burgundy could be ordered for His Majesty; only champagne would do." For the benefit of the Rheims populace on that Royal occasion, four fountains of sparkling champagne flowed at the corner of the Place de l'Hôtel de Ville. To this music then – to the sound of laughter and the popping of champagne corks – the courts of Louis xv and Louis xvi went on their care-free way. To this music too, in 1789 they perished.

When the Revolution broke out, half a dozen firms in Rheims were producing champagne, of which the Sillerys were the most prominent. That they had brought champagne to the court of France was in itself enough to damn them in the eyes of the Revolutionaries. To make matters worse, the last owner of the Sillery vineyards before the Revolution was the Maréchale D'Estrées, the only child of the sixth Marquis de Sillery. This able and domineering woman, who was continuously involved in litigation with the burgesses of Rheims, was hated for the heartless way in which she treated her peasants. As a wine-maker, however, she excelled. She greatly improved the Sillery vineyards by spreading them three times a year with her discovery, the "black cinders" from the mountain of Rheims; and she perfected the blending methods invented by Dom Pérignon. In 1775, her annual income from champagne was £100,000, and in her cellars lay 60,000 bottles.

She died before the Revolution, which was just as well for her. The Revolutionaries pillaged her château in 1790, and tore down the panelling simply because it bore her coat-of-arms. She would certainly have been guillotined – a fate which was reserved for her unfortunate heir, the Comte de Genlis to whom, in default of direct descendants, she had bequeathed the Sillery marquisate and vineyards. Unlike her, he was a model landlord with his peasants, but like her an accomplished agronomist. The English traveller Arthur Young in his *Travels in France*, written just before the Revolution, said that the Comte de Genlis was "the greatest wine-farmer in all Champagne". The Count was still improving his vineyards and property when the Revolution over-took him. In 1793 he was accused of "intelligence with foreigners and émigrés" and executed. His vineyards were sequestrated as national property, and the marquisate of Sillery was extinguished, there being no male heir.

Under the Consulate his son-in-law, the Comte de Valence, bought back much of the property, including the pillaged château. But he possessed little of the ability of his predecessors, and in 1821 he sold his vineyards to M. Jean-Remy Moët (ancestor of the well-known contemporary firm of Moët et Chandon). For some years it seemed that the fame of Sillery champagne would survive the extinction of the family. Such was the magic attached to the name that even the characters in Thackeray's novels thirty years later were drinking "Sillery", which was almost a synonym for "champagne". But by the end of the nineteenth century the lovely name, which had once seemed immortal, was barely known to champagne drinkers. Had fate been kinder, the Marquesses of Sillery would still be today the greatest of the champagne makers; few other wine firms in the world have had as illustrious an origin.

2

The Champagne Widows

No business in the world can have been as much influenced by the female sex as that of champagne. If we think of the *Veuve Joyeuse* with a glass in her hand, we also think of the *Veuve Clicquot* as the young widow who inherited a modest business at her husband's early death, which she transferred in two decades into one of the first wine firms in Europe. Nor was the *Veuve Clicquot* the only "champagne widow". Among other widows who displayed a commercial ability equal to, if not surpassing, that of their smartest male competitors were, the *Veuve Heidsieck* (widowed 1835), the *Veuve Pommery* (widowed 1858), the *Veuve Roederer* (widowed 1932) – and in our own time the *Veuves Bollinger* and *Pol-Roger*, who are still today at the head of their firms. It seems there is something in the air of Champagne which kills the men off early, and then infuses the women with this androgynous potency.

The greatest of them all, their prototype and paragon, was undoubtedly the *Veuve Clicquot* whose husband died in 1805 when she was twenty-three. Sixty years later, at her death, she had become the uncrowned Queen of Champagne and an international celebrity. The well-known portrait at the end of her life shows her enthroned on a settee in billowing taffeta. The broad, determined mouth, the prominent nose and sagacious eyes, may well seem to us today associated more with the City of London than with the frilly lace cap and many-tiered crinoline she is wearing. These masterful features were doubtless the result of half a century of barter and dickering in the Champagne trade, for the early portraits depict her in a very different way – the small

8

frame and delicate features of the shy, retiring wife she was until her husband, François Clicquot, died in 1805.

She was born Nicole-Barbe Ponsardin in 1777 in Rheims, the daughter of a meritorious textile manufacturer. He had taken an official part in the coronation of Louis XVI, and when the Revolution broke out he hastily withdrew his daughter from the Convent of the Abbaye Royale where she was at school; he clad her in clogs and a drugget, and placed her with something less regal, the family of a seamstress who was devoted to his family. Here she spent the revolutionary years in relative tranquillity. She must have heard the drums summoning volunteers to join the army of Kellermann, and seen the Phrygian bonnets in the streets chanting the Marseillaise; but the echoes of Paris resounded only faintly in Rheims. Nicole-Barbe Ponsardin knew little of the Terror, or the Directoire which followed, with the new female arbiters of taste, Mesdames Tallien and Beauharnais, the *Incroyables* setting the fashion. Like any good bourgeois child of her time she waited deferentially until a suitable husband came along. He came in 1799, François Clicquot, the son of a Rheims clothier. Religious marriage being still proscribed in the nihilist state, theirs was celebrated by an *assermenté* priest in a wine-cellar – a portent surely of things to come.

Her young husband François Clicquot worked in his father's clothier business, but he had become more interested in expanding their small vineyard, from which they sold champagne to a limited clientele, friends and business acquaintances. The son believed that big markets lay outside France for sparkling wine (which had been in existence only a century, and was still unknown abroad). On his business trips to Switzerland, Bavaria and Austria, he opened up these markets. His father gradually withdrew from an active part in the firm; by the end of the century François Clicquot had abandoned textiles entirely, and was concentrating on wine. By 1805, the year of his death, he had increased the champagne sales tenfold, particularly in central Europe. Here he was ably assisted by an energetic young German he had discovered, Herr Bohne, who was a first-class salesman. François Clicquot's marriage with Nicole-Barbe Ponsardin had produced a daughter, and a happy family future seemed assured. Then in November 1805, he contracted a malignant fever which carried him off in fifteen days. He was aged twenty-eight.

The loss of the efficient son, on whom his father had increasingly relied, together with a particularly bad harvest that year, determined old Clicquot to sell the business; and negotiations with other firms were begun. But here for the first time, his widowed daughter-in-law made her presence felt. She suggested that, as her late husband had put so much of himself into the new venture, it would profane his memory to transfer it away from the family. If her father-in-law was determined to withdraw, she was prepared to run the firm herself. After some hesitation he agreed, even offering a small sum of capital for the initial period. But he soon realised that she was entirely self-reliant, for the delicate features of the young woman concealed a strong will, a commercial judgement and a remarkable head for figures.

The decision in 1806, with all Europe at war, was courageous. The business was in its infancy; its customers were chiefly foreigners, many of them inaccessible in time of war; the employees were all male, unaccustomed to taking orders from a woman; and until now, she had concerned herself exclusively with the care of her daughter. Moreover, at the opening of the nineteenth century in a provincial city like Rheims, there was much shaking of heads at such flouting of feminine decorum. Women of the working classes might be employed in commerce, but "ladies" were not expected to compete with men on the boards of directors.

None of this appears to have daunted Nicole-Barbe Clicquot who had no intention of hiding her talents under her widow's weeds. She immediately styled the firm, "*Veuve Clicquot-Ponsardin et Cie*", incorporating her maiden name. She was well aware of the ability of her husband's German associate, M. Bohne, whom she took into her full confidence. The sales ability of this red-haired, corpulent and intensely active little man, is evident in an early letter he wrote to Mme Clicquot about a prospective rich customer: "Lavish on him when he arrives," he advised, "every civility and pleasure that Rheims can provide. Take entire possession of his person. Ensure that you and your friends occupy every hour of his day. He must have all his meals with you – or competitors will get hold of him."

Of another prospective client, he wrote, "He is a man entirely without education, a former tinker. Yet I commend him to you most warmly. Take complete possession of him, lodge him, feed him, fête him, flatter his vanity. Let him visit our cellars (but not in working hours). He will tell you some things that are true, some that are arrant lies; he will yawn, appear bored – but if you can surround him with that amiability which is a part of your character, and *if you cling onto him like a spider to a fly*, HE WILL BUY !"

At the outset Mme Clicquot decided to concentrate on eastern Europe and Russia. She sent M. Bohne to St Petersburg, from where he wrote characteristically, "I learn privately that the Czarina is pregnant. What a blessing for us if she gives birth to a son ! Oceans of champagne will flow in this vast country ! Not a word of this to anyone at home, of course, or all our competitors will be running north."

In the early days, not all Mme Clicquot's ventures were successful. Indeed, the first was a disaster. In 1806, she despatched 60,000 bottles to Amsterdam, from where they were to be transported by sea to customers in Danzig and Königsberg. This was on the morrow of Trafalgar and Austerlitz, when the English Navy's blockade of the European coast made the normal sea passage impossible. The bottles were inadequately stored while awaiting the lifting of the blockade. The wine deteriorated, and Mme Clicquot had no alternative but to instruct her agent in Amsterdam to sell it at any price he could get. This was so low that she then had to pawn her jewellery. But she was never dismayed. Hearing that, although French ships could no longer venture on the high seas, the American flag had immunity from the English blockade, she henceforth organised her transport of champagne in American bottoms.

She now engaged more travellers to sell her wines on the continent, and was soon one of the few champagne dealers during the Napoleonic wars with agencies abroad. Communications both on land and sea were execrable; everything depended on the initiative of the head of the firm. It is some measure of this initiative, as well as of her agent's devotion to her, that they tolerated every privation, travelling over appalling roads, frequently molested by the ubiquitous soldiery, putting up at inns which were full of fleas and lice. One of them wrote that he had to buy a carriage, not to make travel more comfortable, but to sleep in, as all the inns were shut, and the peasants' rooms infested with vermin. Once when M. Bohne was running the gauntlet before the British navy, he was wrecked off the coast of Heligoland – in his words, "an island of pirates and robbers, of which it were better that no one had ever heard the name." Understandably, he had a poor opinion of the English. "May the genius of our great Emperor," he wrote to Mme Clicquot, "rid humanity of these maritime hell-cats, and so give peace to the world! May the English spend the winter at the bottom of the beastly sea they control, rather than on their iniquitous isle, the lair of manhood's murderers." He even hoped to use champagne to corrupt their habits. "May the good God give us peace!" he said, "so that we can take vengeance on their throats for the evil they have done us – by giving them over to total drunkenness."*

While these agents travelled all over Eastern Europe, Mme Clicquot directed affairs at home in Rheims, and from her small country property at nearby Oger. Although she had a gift for organisation, she only intervened among her subordinates when it was absolutely necessary – always encouraging, advising, stating her requirements clearly and simply. She never interfered with the travellers, to whom she left complete freedom to take the necessary decisions on the spot. She dealt with all the business correspondence herself. The clarity of her letters, the punctuality of her replies, the concern she displayed for the problems of her employees, their private lives, the health of their families – all this contributed to the reputation of the House of Clicquot. During the long months when she was in Rheims, she took personal direction of the cellars. Every day she interviewed Jacob, the head

*He did not know how near the truth he was. The English today are the greatest of foreign champagne drinkers.

cellarer, and discussed the condition of the wines, the state of the *mousse* and the best dates for delivery.

Her great technical contribution to the champagne industry was her method for removing the deposit, which clouded the wine. Each bottle was held neck downward and tapped at the bottom to detach the sediment, the operation being constantly repeated until the deposit had settled in the neck. It was driven out by the explosion which followed the removal of the cork. She further simplified this process by placing the bottles in sloping racks, and having them turned every day. The result was, as she proudly proclaimed, to make her wine "more limpid than any other champagne".

In the competitive male champagne world, she also showed that she, too, had teeth. One day she received a letter from a friend informing her that a Metz wine merchant called Robin was exporting wine to Russia under her trade mark, the letters V.C.P on the cork (Veuve Clicquot-Ponsardin). Her informant added, "He has just sent another 135 cases, each with 60 bottles. I tell you of this, because I fear it will damage the reputation you have built up."

Mme Clicquot reacted sharply, with a short letter of one line, "I intend to make an example of the rascal"; while to the Public Prosecutor in Metz she wrote, "You will, I am sure, appreciate that it is high time this form of brigandage ceased. There must be no mercy for this kind of scoundrel." The "scoundrel" Robin, on being indicted, took flight to Frankfurt. It seemed that nothing could be done, but she continued to press for a verdict in his absence, offering to pay all the legal expenses. Eventually the courts, under her continuous pressure, tried the case *in absentia*; the counterfeiter was sentenced to ten years' hard labour and to be branded on the right shoulder with the letter F (*fugitif*). From his hiding place in Germany he wrote her, imploring her to use her influence in favour of leniency if he returned to his native land – because, he explained, the letters V.C.P on his corks stood for Véritable ChamPagne. If he expected all women to be tender-hearted he was mistaken. She replied, "Your letter has reached me.

If you are innocent return to Metz, and there purge your refusal to appear in court."

At the beginning of 1814, Rheims was surrounded by the Allied armies and the fall of the Empire was imminent. On 26 January, Mme Clicquot's father, the Baron Ponsardin (as Mayor of Rheims he had been ennobled by Napoleon), received the order to evacuate the administration. He invited Mme Clicquot and her daughter to accompany him. But she refused to leave Rheims; she intended to stay, she said, in the hope that her presence would protect her cellars. To a Parisian cousin she wrote, "All goes extremely badly here. For days I have been walling up my cellars; but I doubt whether this will prevent theft and pillage by the soldiery. Anyway, if I am ruined when the foreign armies arrive, I suppose I must resign myself and work to keep alive. I do not regret my past days of prosperity, except for my daughter. It would have been far better for her if the French defeat had occurred five or six years earlier, for then she would not have known the good life, which she will now greatly miss. But I shall try to do without everything, and will sacrifice everything so that she may not be unhappy."

It was amid these inauspicious conditions, with the Allied armies at the gate, when all seemed lost, that Mme Cliquot and the egregious Bohne achieved their greatest feat – and this by taking another risk. France and Russia were still officially at war, and the import of French wine into Russia was forbidden. But peace would soon be signed, and whoever imported the first consignment of champagne would gain a considerable advantage over his competitors. Mme Clicquot took the risk of sending Bohne in a ship loaded with champagne to Königsberg from where he was to smuggle it over the frontier so that it would be available in Russia when peace was signed.

Ten thousand bottles were accordingly sent to Rouen, where they were shipped on the *Gebroeders*, a 75-ton Dutch vessel which Mme Cliquot had hired for the purpose, and on which she stipulated no other merchandise was to be carried. M. Bohne did not relish the month's journey; he wrote to her, "My cabin is no bigger than an alcove, and there is no bed. I shall sleep on the floor. If I die on the way, I commend you to my good wife and daughter." He had to provide his own food – ham, biscuits, vinegar, bacon and apples. When he arrived in Königsberg a month later, after a hideous voyage on which "bed-bugs two inches long have drunk half the blood in my body", he heard the gratifying news that the ban on French wine had just been lifted, and that Russia had opened her frontiers. The House of Clicquot had stolen a month's march on its competitors. Mme Clicquot immediately despatched a second, and then a third, vessel loaded with champagne. M. Bohne wrote from St Petersburg, "They had forgotten what it was. You are becoming as famous here as M. Maille is in Paris for his mustard and vinegar."

This Russian venture was the turning-point in the fortunes of the firm. After this, Mme Clicquot abandoned central European markets altogether and concentrated entirely on Russia, where she soon had a monopoly. To drink champagne in Russia was to drink "Clicquot"; the words were synonymous. Soon Russian literature was paying tribute to her wine. In Pushkin's story, *The Shot*, the hero has, "Two or three dishes prepared by a retired soldier, and the champagne of Clicquot flowed like water." In Lermontov's *A Hero of Our Times*, the hero states, "My champagne proved an even more magnetic attraction to him than even his girl-friend's pretty eyes." Merimée says that champagne in Russia was known as "Klikoskoe"; and Pushkin compares the Clicquot wines to the fountain of Hippocrene where the poets went for inspiration.*

The Russians became clients of a somewhat different order when, with the other Allied troops, they occupied Champagne after the war. Their soldiers had never drunk Madame Clicquot's wine, as supplied to her well-to-do customers in St Petersburg. Tradition relates that the Cossacks used to pour champagne into buckets and share it with their horses. The Russian officers soon realised however that they were drinking at a charmed fountain, which excited a thirst that could not be quenched. Mme Clicquot was informed

*Champagne is not imported into Soviet Russia today – as the French pointedly reminded their ex-client at a dinner given for Mr Gromyko, the Russian Foreign Minister, at Geneva in 1959. The *Figaro* reported, "M Couve de Murville was careful to include on the menu – which had on it a *suprême de sole à la Cherbourg* – a Veuve Clicquot, which occupies a certain place in Russian literature, particularly in the works of Pushkin."

on one occasion that drunken Russian officers were swilling champagne in her cellars. "Let them go on drinking!" was her comment. "They will pay!" She was right. In the decades after the war, millions of bottles specially fortified to a strength and sweetness suited to the hyperborean climate were annually despatched to Russia from the House of Clicquot. From this influx of sparkling wine in such quantities into the frozen empire of the Czar, civilisation there may be said to date. If Peter the Great had drunk champagne instead of corn-brandy, the country might have become Europeanised earlier. To drink it in Russia was now recognised as a step towards a liberal education. It was said that in upper-class Russian society, whenever champagne was given at a dinner party, the host was careful to throw the windows open, so that the popping of the corks might announce the fact to his neighbours.

With the return of European peace, Mme Clicquot's business continued to prosper, and by 1821 the demand for her champagne exceeded the supply by 100,000 bottles. In the words of Evelyn Waugh, "Champagne is the wine of celebration and ostentation." As the years of peace followed one another, Mme Clicquot's corks popped even more often at soirées, bachelor supper parties, even at military outposts and ship-building yards.* In June 1822 she felt prosperous enough to branch out into another line of business; she opened a bank in Rheims under the title of *"Veuve Clicquot-Ponsardin et Cie"*, and soon had banking clients in Amsterdam, St Petersburg and Vienna. That prosperity did not induce complacency or blunt her business acumen is revealed by the letter she wrote to English friends just before the coronation of Charles x in Rheims:

As you know, the brother of your King, the Duke of Northumberland, is to attend the Coronation as Ambassador Extraordinary. There can be no doubt that during his visit to our town the Prince and his suite will consume a great deal of champagne, and will need a banker to supply them with money. If you can find a way of offering my services to the

*From Preface to *The Life and Times of Madame Veuve Clicquot* by Jacqueline Caraman-Chimay.

noble Lord [sic], either directly or through the intermediary
of some influential personage of your acquaintance, I believe
he might accept them; in that case I would pay you a good
commission on the wine I sell him.

Two years later she embarked on yet another venture, this time
in wool. The firm's archives still contain letters she wrote to sheep-
farmers in Burgundy, Berry and Picardy ordering their wool to sell
in Rheims. There are also letters from her to Rheims textile merchants offering to procure wool for them from Hanover, Austria,
Moravia and Switzerland. She also bought a large spinning-mill
at Esslingen, near Stuttgart.

Having spent the last twenty years of her life in such a frenzy
of commerce, Mme Clicquot now felt she could turn her attention
to domestic affairs. The time had come, she felt, for her daughter
Clementine, aged twenty-two, to marry; and in keeping with the
grande bourgeoise tradition of France, she planned a marriage into
the aristocracy. She was now known as one of the richest merchants
in Rheims; and the eligible young men and their families all
demanded huge dowries. After much bargaining, she accepted
Comte Louis de Chévigné, a penniless but good-looking scion of
the *ancien régime*; in the best tradition, all his immediate ancestors
had been guillotined. He appears to have made her daughter
happy, although he was extravagant and a reckless gambler.
When he was not spending Mme Clicquot's money, he composed
bad verse and attended parades of the Rheims National Guard,
of which he became an honorary colonel. He persuaded his mother-
in-law to buy the ruined château of Boursault, restore it to its
former glory and use it as the family's summer residence.

Until now, Mme Clicquot had spent her few moments of relaxation in her unpretentious country house at Oger. She now had
to pay the bills for the extensive restoration work at Boursault,
with its towers and turrets, marquetry panelling, chandeliers,
Aubusson carpets and huge Burgundian stone fireplaces – in the
words of Patrick Forbes, "all rivalling in magnificence anything
produced by the sixteenth-century artists on the banks of the
Loire". It appears, however, that with time her thrifty nature

became reconciled to it, for it was here that she lived in grand style until her death, and where the legend of the uncrowned Queen of Champagne was born.

The only other setback (if the Comte de Chévigné can be called a setback) sustained by the firm in these years of prosperity was the death of M. Bohne. But Mme Clicquot with her quick eye for talent soon discovered another efficient German, Edouard Werlé, who took over the functions of M. Bohne. In 1828, after being in the firm only a year, he saved it from disaster. He considered that Mme Clicquot had gone too far by branching out into the other domains, banking and wool. In 1828, his fears were justified.

The Parisian bank Poupart, with which her bank and firm was closely associated, went bankrupt. Immediately, every Clicquot creditor demanded their deposits – some coming for them in person to the door of the firm. The young M. Werlé did not hesitate an instant. Without even informing Mme Clicquot, he went post-haste to Paris to see M. Rougemont de Lowenberg, another banker with whom the firm dealt on a smaller scale; he asked him to lend them two millions to meet the more pressing demands of their creditors. The bland self-assurance and confidence of the young man was such that M. Rougemont allowed him a million in cash and another million on credit.

That evening M. Werlé returned to Rheims, and the next day set up a department in the office with which he paid every one of the creditors who demanded their deposits. The news of these repayments quickly spread in the town, where people assumed that the credit of the Clicquot firm was not as badly shaken as they had at first supposed. Not only did the demands for repayment cease, but within a few days deposits were being paid in again. Mme Clicquot expressed her gratitude for this courageous act by promoting M. Werlé immediately to the chief position under her in the firm. In July 1831, he became a partner and took French nationality.

His prestige and influence in the firm increased, while that of her son-in-law, Louis de Chévigné, diminished, as his debts increased. Mme Clicquot was thankful at least now to be able to confront his incessant demands for more money with the severe countenance of the German businessman, Werlé. Henceforth, when the gambling debts had gone too far, Louis de Chévigné had to explain them away to the senior partner, instead of wheedling the money out of a mother-in-law. He also began dabbling in politics, in favour of a restored monarchy in the intervals of writing scabrous poetry. He published his verses, *Les Contes Rémois*, on the lines of La Fontaine's *Fables*, which he persuaded Meissonnier to illustrate. His mother-in-law was so shocked by their contents that she bought up every copy she could lay hands on, so that the name of her daughter should not be compromised; whereupon Chévigné published several more editions. She again ordered her agents to buy them up and destroy them. In this way, he pocketed a further sum of money. Louis de Chévigné's attitude towards his marriage appears to have been quite simply that he had lent his name to a pack of bourgeois who had a talent for making money; he did not possess that talent himself, but he had a talent for spending it.

However, he gave his mother-in-law one thing she wanted, a posterity associated with some of the greatest names of France. For her grand-daughter, Anne de Mortemart, married the Duc d'Uzès, by whom she had three children who later became, respectively, the Duc d'Uzès, the Duchesse de Luynes and the Duchesse de Briasac.

Mme Clicquot died at Boursault on 29 July 1866, aged eighty-nine. She left the firm to M. Werlé, and some of the vineyards to her descendants. At Werlé's death, the firm passed to his son, who married a grand-daughter of the Duc de Montebello. After the death of the second Werlé at the beginning of the twentieth century, the firm was managed for over forty years by his son-in-law, the Comte Bertrand de Mum, and then for another generation by the Prince Jean Caraman-Chimay. Today it is run by Comte Bertrand de Vogüé, who is married to the Comte de Mum's daughter.

We can still see Mme Clicquot today in the cellars of the firm in Rheims, where a shadow masque in period costume is enacted for the benefit of visitors – the widow passing by candle-light before her wines to confer, as she did daily in her lifetime, with her faithful cellarer, Jacob.

To describe the careers of all the other champagne widows who proved to be good businesswomen would be repetitive; and to select only one or two would be invidious. Those incidents in their careers which distinguish them from Mme Clicquot – and from one another – may however be briefly mentioned.

Mme Pommery was left a widow in 1858 when she was thirty-nine, at a much later age than Mme Clicquot. She, too, had never taken part in commerce before; but she immediately gave a new direction to the firm's exports by deciding that the best potential market was England. She also had a flair for choosing energetic lieutenants, often from humble origins. Such a man was M. Hubinet, who was familiar with the business world of England, where she sent him for five years to develop the market. She also conceived the novel idea of flattering her prospective British clients by building her establishment outside Rheims on the lines of an English stately home. For models, she took the houses of two of her most distinguished customers, the Duke of Argyll and the Earl of Haddington – Inverary Castle and Mellerstein. A mile outside Rheims her creation stands, a group of buildings half brick, half stone, some with the round corner towers of Inverary, others with the plain castellated façade of Robert Adam's Mellerstein – a bizarre and, to some people, a hideous, spectacle, Victorian Gothic in the gentle landscape of Champagne. Nor did she forget that an English stately home must have a park. The gardens are planted with trees, flower-beds and English lawns. Within ten years of inheriting the firm at her widowhood, she had established the English as her best customers.

One of her most remarkable achievements was the conversion for publicity purposes of the *crayères* or chalk-pits which underlie the whole of the Rheims-Epernay area into the most spectacular cellars in Champagne. These cellars, which date from Roman times – quarried by slave labour for the chalk blocks used in building the city of Rheims, or *Durocortorum*, as it was known then –

form a subterranean network two hundred miles in length, capable of storing 250 million bottles of champagne. Mme Pommery decided to exploit their picturesque, if somewhat sinister, reputation. Not content with galleries which are remarkable for their seemingly never-ending length, she introduced arches into them in a variety of styles – Roman, Norman, Gothic – naming them after the great champagne cities of the world, London, New York, Rome, Stockholm, Buenos Aires. She then commissioned a Champenois artist, Navlet, to carve huge bas-reliefs on the walls. The chalk proved an excellent medium for the sculptor's chisel, and the bas-reliefs are as striking today as when they were carved – one, for instance, depicting a rollicking Regency *petit souper*, entitled *Le champagne au XVIII siècle*, and another the *Fête de Bacchus*. She completed the work with a triumphal staircase down to the depths, twelve feet wide with 116 steps.

Like Mme Clicquot when she became rich, Mme Pommery married her daughters into the French aristocracy, to one of its most ancient families, the Polignacs, members of which have been connected with the firm ever since. At one point, it was rumoured that the firm was running into financial difficulties and, as in the case already related of Mme Clicquot and M. Werlé, there was a run on the deposits. Her method of scotching the rumour was more original than M. Werlé's. She had read that French newspapers were criticising on patriotic grounds the impending sale to America of Millet's famous painting *Les Glaneuses*. She accordingly bought it for 300,000 francs and presented it to the Louvre. Thus at one stroke, she dispelled the rumours and obtained wide publicity for her patriotic action.

A portrait of this formidable lady shows her as more of a *femme du monde* than Mme Clicquot – the elegant black silk dress, the narrow collar with a gold brooch in the centre, on her head a blue toque with a black mantilla hanging from the shoulder. The hands with their long pointed fingers and the finely curled nostrils suggest breeding. The lips are slightly curled at the corners as if about to smile. It is hard from this picture to discern the efficient business woman she must have been.

At the centenary of the firm in 1936 the Marquis de Polignac, her grandson, did homage to her in these words:

I seem to see her again as I used to when a child, going to kiss her in the early morning before setting off to school – seeing her seated at her desk surrounded by a heap of files and dossiers. She would have already written in her own hand a number of letters while preparing for the day's work ahead, which she would fill with her indefatigable energy. At other times I saw her in the office of her *chef des caves*, M. Lambert, much concerned with the working conditions of her employees, for she was fundamentally warm-hearted and charitable.

The most picturesque figure in the champagne trade today is Madame Lily Bollinger, the widow of Jacques Bollinger. A member of an old Touraine family, she assumed control of the firm when her husband died in 1941. There could hardly have been a less auspicious moment for a woman – or indeed for any successor – to have such responsibility thrust upon her. The firm's premises in Ay had been severely bombed in 1940, and three arduous years of German occupation still lay ahead. But Madame Bollinger guided her inheritance through the war years with the greatest skill and perseverance – as she still does today.

Sheer hard work is the secret of her success. Every morning she is at her desk by nine o'clock, riding to the office from her château on a bicycle. Almost every day she is hostess in her elegant dining-room to agents and friends from all over the world. Then there are her trips abroad. She visits New York annually, and London several times a year. On these occasions the clothes she wears are made for her by one of the great French couturiers. But to the citizens of Champagne she is more familiar in her tweeds in winter, or a simple cotton dress in summer, riding to work on a bicycle.

A wine merchant told me that once, when he was invited to lunch at her château, he found half a dozen other guests seated at her table. He started making conversation to his neighbour, a lady who did not reply and looked at him, it seemed, disapprovingly. He gradually became aware that no one else was talking; and it was not until Madame Bollinger spoke that the conversation became general. He was later informed that it was not customary at meals for anyone to speak until Madame Bollinger saw fit to open the conversation.

The 1972 was the twentieth vintage *cuvée* whose production she had personally supervised. Such is her knowledge and experience of viticulture that she will always take an independent line, in conflict with all accepted notions. For instance, in recent years most of the champagne firms have been modernising their plants with metal vats for the first fermentation and storage. She maintains that there is nothing to beat the old wood cask. What matters, she says, are the traditional, well-tried methods.

I am indebted to Mr Patrick Forbes and his excellent book on *Champagne: The wine, the land, the people,* for a significant comment on her character. He recalls how, at a large dinner party which she gave in her château for a group of British wine merchants, she handed round the coffee, the marc and the cognac herself, mentioning in passing that she had been out since six in the morning inspecting the vines. The hour, Forbes says, was very late; it would have been easy for the waiters who had served the magnificent dinner to serve the coffee and *digestifs* too; but "When you are young and were yourself in bed at eight or nine in the morning, it is quite something to have been offered your coffee and your marc or your cognac by a great lady of Champagne who was out in her vineyard at six."

Another remarkable champagne widow alive today is Camille Olry-Roederer. In 1932 her husband left her in his will his champagne firm, his large estates in Normandy, and one of the finest stables of trotting-horses in Europe. In each of these domains, she has proved the equal of her husband. Many stories are told about her forceful character. She hoodwinked the German in the Second World War into giving her a larger ration of sugar than she needed for making her champagne – in order to pass most of it on to her workers. She wears a man-sized wrist-watch "to give masculine authority", even when dressed in a Dior garment, and ear-rings composed of clusters of gold grapes, and bracelets of miniature gold champagne bottles. She has always shown great concern for the welfare of her cart-horses, and has invented a special method for washing their hooves.

Some male champagne competitors are jealous of her ingenious publicity devices. They complain that no sooner have they started to make progress in a foreign market than Madame Roederer appears and enters one of her champion trotting-horses in the local races. She arrives for the race and astounds everyone at the subsequent celebration party with her magnificent diamonds; after that, everyone wishes to drink Roederer champagne. The Lord Mayor of London served it in 1956 to Messrs Khrushchev and Bulganin when they attended a banquet at the Mansion House.

The last living "champagne widow" whom I met was Madame Odette Pol-Roger, great-grand-daughter of Sir Richard Wallace, of Wallace Collection fame. (She and her two beautiful sisters are known to all Paris as "The Wallace Collection".) Since the death of her husband eighteen years ago, she has been living alone, mostly at Epernay. The success of widows in running champagne firms she explains in terms of nationality. "French women like living alone," she says. "Contrast this with the Americans. For an American woman, it is a dishonour not to marry again. It is an admission of dreadful failure. For some English women, too, I think. But there we are more intelligent; we do not mind living alone."

She is fully aware however that, unlike the other champagne widows who are responsible for the present success of their firms, the greatest credit in hers must go to her late father-in-law, M. Maurice Pol-Roger, the real "Father of the Firm". She admires him, she said, for the way in which he combined running the firm with being Mayor of Epernay and devoting so much time to sport. "He would go off regularly," she said, "on fishing expeditions each spring, shoot grouse in Scotland in August and wild boar in Champagne in the late autumn. He killed 525 boar in his lifetime. Once when he was asked how he had any time for business, he replied, 'Primarily between saying my prayers in the morning,

and the time I go to shoot.' " This appears to have been almost
literally true. He used to leave his office at 9.30 am, having spent
a few hours transacting business, change in the car, shoot or fish,
change again in the car, and be back in the office at 5 pm to sign
his correspondence.

She also admired him for his behaviour in the First World War.
Champagne suffered more than any of the other wine-growing
regions of France during four years of German occupation. When
the Germans arrived on 4 September 1914, M. Pol-Roger was
Mayor of Epernay. The town was soon crammed with refugees,
the wounded, German soldiers and French prisoners; Prince William
of Prussia, the fourth son of the Kaiser, and General von Moltke
set up their headquarters in Epernay. To add to the confusion,
the police and other civic authorities had fled just before the
German arrival, taking with them the municipal funds. As there
was no paper money, it was impossible to buy anything. M.
Maurice Pol-Roger rose to the occasion. He issued small paper notes,
signed and guaranteed by his firm, announcing that anyone who
refused them as legal tender would be arrested. In this way – such
was the inhabitants' confidence in the name of Pol Roger – he
saved the day. In recognition of this and other war-time services,
he was presented after the war with a bound volume containing
the signature of every citizen who had remained behind in Epernay
during the German occupation.

Unlike the other champagne widows, Madame Pol-Roger is less
concerned today with the running of the firm in Epernay than
with propagating its name abroad. Endowed with great beauty,
she does this effortlessly simply by being present at any reception
given in New York, London or Paris, where everyone turns to
look at her. The most distinguished person who "turned to look"
was Sir Winston Churchill, who met her in 1944 at the British
Embassy in Paris. Thereafter, he would drink only Pol Roger
champagne, and he even christened one of his race horses "Odette
Pol-Roger". It won four races. The bound volume of his war
memoirs which Sir Winston gave to Madame Pol-Roger was
inscribed :

Cuvée de Réserve
Mise en bouteille
Au Château de Chartwell*

When Sir Winston died, she added a black border to the Pol Roger bottles in his memory – as we buy them today.

*Translation: First growth bottled at the Château Chartwell.

3

Jean-Remy Moët and Comte
Robert de Vogüé

It might be supposed from the previous chapter that champagne is the exclusive preserve of the female sex, that it is virtually impossible to make it unless you are a widow. The widows have been chosen and described in some detail, because they are the most picturesque members of the trade. But Moët et Chandon, which has always been run by males has had an equally eventful history, and is today by far the biggest of the champagne firms. Until 1962, when it became a *Société Anonyme*, it was one of the largest businesses of any kind in France, entirely owned and run by one family.

It was founded by Claude Moët in Epernay in the first half of the eighteenth century, and it appears almost immediately to have prospered – for one of his first customers was Madame de Pompadour. In the firm's archives are her orders for two hundred bottles at a time, to be sent to Compiègne in the month of May, before the court moved there.

In the same year, Claude Moët made his first foreign sale – two *poinçons* of champagne to a Mr Grupty of London. Between 1755 and 1791 he opened markets in Germany, Spain and Russia. In 1780, the firm sent its first traveller to England, M. Jeanson, who wrote, "How the taste of this country has changed in the last ten years! Almost everywhere they ask for sparkling champagne – and we must monopolise the market."

In 1791 Claude Moët died leaving the business to the commercial genius who – as we shall see on several occasions in this study of wine families – seems essential at some point in the burgeoning of a great firm, to his son Jean-Remy Moët. It was an untimely moment for a young man to assume such responsibility, with the Terror at its height. He was quick to insert on the bills of lading and invoices to his customers the word "Citizen" before their names; this probably saved him from the scaffold. But he had little sympathy with the Jacobins; as soon as the Directoire was established, he switched back to the normal courtesy titles. Under the Consulate he became Mayor of Epernay, and in 1804 when Napoleon was proclaimed Emperor, he launched into a ten-year period of giddy business and social success, such as no other wine-maker in history can have had. At the basis of this lay his friendship with Napoleon.

Quite apart from his admiration for the Emperor, which amounted almost to idolatry, Jean-Remy Moët could only benefit financially from the Imperial favour; and Napoleon, who appears to have had a genuine affection for him, also found the association advantageous. For Jean-Remy's cellars lay on the direct road from Paris to Germany, on which Napoleon was to spend so much of his life. "History," writes Patrick Forbes, "records no other monarch blessed with a subject so responsive to the Imperial will that, at a mere hint, he erected at his own expense, not one house to put up Napoleon and his Court, but two."

Jean-Remy commissioned Jean-Baptiste Isabey, the miniaturist and the favourite painter of the *Incroyables* and Napoleonic society, to design, opposite his own house in Epernay, two identical white buildings and the sunken garden and pond with, on the far side, the elegant Rococo orangery. We can still visit these buildings today.

One of the first distinguished visitors to accept Jean-Remy's hospitality was the Empress Josephine. She spent the night of 16 October 1804 in one of these new houses, and returned in 1807 on her way back to Malmaison from Plombières where she had been taking the waters. Plombières was notorious for being as dull and uncomfortable as its waters were salubrious; and we may imagine how much she was looking forward to her bedroom in Epernay overlooking the French garden, the flowing champagne and Jean-Remy's anecdotes. It was said of him that he "never entered a salon without chasing away boredom".

Fresh from his Austrian victories that summer, the Emperor too arrived at Epernay in state. Jean-Remy conducted him round the cellars, through ranks of cellarmen holding lighted candelabras, and explained the intricacies of the *méthode champenoise* in much the same terms as are used by the Moët cellar-guides today. A plaque in the entrance hall of Moët et Chandon's offices commemorates the visit: "On 26 July 1807 Napoleon the Great, Emperor of the French, King of Italy, Protector of the Confederation of the Rhine, honoured Commerce by visiting the cellars of Jean-Remy Moët, Mayor of Epernay, President of the Canton and member of the General Council of the Department, within three weeks of the signature of the Treaty of Tilsit."

Plaques do not record the Emperor's other visits, partly because they were not official, partly because they were so frequent. There are plenty of entries in the firm's archives such as: "The Emperor arrived on 22 September 1808 on his way to Châlons-sur-Marne"; and "The Emperor arrived at 8 pm on 26 October 1809 on his return from Austria", and so on.

In 1811, Jean-Remy entertained the Emperor's brother, Jérôme Bonaparte; but this was an ominous occasion. After placing an order for 6,000 bottles, Jérôme said, "In happier circumstances, I would have taken twice the amount, but I'm afraid the Russians would drink it for me."

"The Russians? ... I don't understand you, Sire," exclaimed Jean-Remy.

"All right, I'll let you into a state secret. In my brother's cabinet, war with Russia has been decided on. It's terrible, terrible! I see no hope of success."

"But Sire ..."

"Yes, I know what you're going to tell me: 'The Emperor's genius overcomes all obstacles!' That's what everyone says.... I only hope I'm wrong. Only time can tell."*

The battles of Berezina and Borodino the following year confirmed Jérôme's predictions.

Just before his abdication at Fontainebleau, Napoleon

*This dialogue is reported by Patrick Forbes in his *The Story of the Maison Moët et Chandon*, 1972.

visited his vintner friend for the last time. It was during this visit that Jean-Remy carried his imperial guest's breakfast up to him in his bedroom, and was rewarded – not for that, but for ten years faithful service – with Napoleon's Cross of the Legion of Honour.

With the fall of Napoleon, it seemed that Jean-Remy's star had set. But business is business; and when the Allied statesmen at the Vienna Congress found Epernay conveniently on their route to Paris, he entertained them equally royally. His guest list in 1815 reads like an index to the Congress: Alexander of Russia, Francis Emperor of Austria, the King of Prussia, the Grand Duke Nicholas of Russia, the Prince of Württemberg, the Prince of Baden, the Duke of Wellington, Marshal Blücher, Prince Metternich. Jean-Remy's ten years of prominence under Napoleon had made him the most famous wine-maker in Europe, and orders for his champagne came pouring in in such profusion that he could hardly satisfy them. The list of his customers between 1814 and 1839 includes an equally dazzling array of names, monarchs and sovereign princes, headed by Queen Victoria, dukes, (fifteen British dukes were among his customers), and many other famous men of the day.

To state that Jean-Remy enjoyed a virtual monopoly in supplying champagne to fashionable circles in England and the Continent during the quarter century that followed Waterloo is not an overstatement. Indeed, Talleyrand hardly exaggerated when he said one night while dining with Jean-Remy in Paris, "My dear friend, you are assured of immortality. I predict that thanks to this cup and its contents, your name will *mousse* far more and far longer than mine."

Jean-Remy's Napoleonic associations do not appear to have antagonised the Bourbons at the Restoration. In 1825 Charles X paid an official visit to the cellars, accompanied by the Duchesse d'Angoulême, Louis XVI's daughter. Over thirty years before, during the royal family's escape from Varennes, she had narrowly avoided being lynched by the mob on the Châlons-Epernay road. Napoleon's remark that "she was the only man in her family" perhaps explains her sang-froid in returning to a place that must have held such terrible associations for her. Seven years later Louise-Philippe, King of the French, visited Jean-Remy on his way to a military parade at Lunéville; he ordered new supplies of champagne for Compiègne and the Tuileries, and asked to see the room where Napoleon had slept in 1814. Jean-Remy kept it exactly as the Emperor had left it.

In 1832 Jean-Remy retired from active direction of the firm, and handed it over to his son, Victor, and his son-in-law, Chandon de Briailles. Since then the firm which had been "Moët et Cie" assumed its present famous name, "Moët et Chandon". He also resigned as Mayor of Epernay, having for several decades handled the town's affairs with the same energy, imagination and business acumen which he had displayed in his firm. During his mayoralty, he was responsible for the new bridge across the Marne, and the building of Epernay's present theatre. One of his actions while the theatre was being built was typical of the man. Hearing that the Théâtre Montansier in Paris, (today the Théâtre du Palais Royal), was in liquidation, he bought all the decorations and accessories, and presented them to Epernay. A great source of pleasure to him in his last days was his 120-acre estate of Romaont. He had bought this, we have already seen, from the bankrupt Sillery estate, and it included forty-four acres of the famous vineyard.

After his death, his heirs greatly expanded the flourishing concern he had left them. They bought up vineyards at almost any prices, and by 1879 had become the greatest vineyard proprietors in Champagne, with a total of 900 acres, including such famous *crus* as Cramant, Le Mesnil, Bouzy, Ay, and Verzenay. They extended their premises on the Avenue de Champagne in Epernay until the buildings covered an area of over twenty acres. But the basis of their fame and fortune continued to be the *"Brut Impérial"*, whose name and crowns on the label commemorate the Napoleonic connection.

Lastly, the connection of the firm with Richard Wagner may be mentioned. M. Paul Chandon who took over the firm after Jean-Remy's death was not unworthy of his great father-in-law. A keen music-lover, he used to invite Wagner to stay at 9 Avenue de Champagne. After the failure of *Tannhäuser* in Paris, Wagner wrote to him one of the finest tributes ever paid to champagne by a great artist:

> Most esteemed friend ... I could never have risen above the bitterness I have been feeling these last few weeks if I had not constantly recalled your friendship.... Believe me, that magnificent wine you sent to my house proved my sole means of mending my broken spirits, and I cannot speak too highly of the effect it had on me at the moment when there was so much I wanted to forget. It had the same effect on the small group of friends who stood by me. I assure you that for several evenings in succession, I remembered with nostalgia the pleasant impression it left with me ...

Another letter Paul Chandon received from Wagner was written from the Villa Tribschen near Lucerne in 1868:

> A line, most honoured friend, to ask you to send a consignment from your world-famous cellars to my modest refuge in Switzerland, where it looks as though I shall be stranded for a long time. I should like for my personal consumption, a good champagne, not the type for ladies but something hearty for men. I am sure that with your usual kindness you, who are so eminently qualified to do so, will select the quality for me. Please send me 30 bottles and 100 half-bottles. Draw a bill on me, payable at the end of the half-year. If it would give you pleasure to be present at a performance of one of my new works, I invite you to Munich in mid-June. I shall never forget the part you took in that ill-fated performance of *Tannhäuser* in Paris.

The last letter in their correspondence is a little different in tone, because the Franco-German war, which was so disastrous for Champagne, had already taken place. It was dated "Bayreuth. 25 May 1875": "Since the war I have had no champagne, as I was afraid of offending you by asking for your assistance, to which I have been accustomed for so long. I now venture to renew our former relations by asking you to instruct your house to send me 50 big and 100 half-bottles of the excellent produce of your vineyards."

As Mr Patrick Forbes says, Wagner's reticence was understandable, because M. Paul Chandon had suffered greatly during the war. It had fallen to him as municipal councillor to collect the 200,000 franc indemnity imposed by the Germans on Epernay in 1870. When this proved impossible because so many of the inhabitants had fled, taking their savings with them, he had – to save his life – to make out a cheque for that sum on his personal account. On several occasions, he was forced by the Prussian railway authorities to act as a hostage against sabotage on their trains, riding beside the driver, getting covered with soot in the process. Then there was the incident at the hospital for 600 beds in Epernay, which M. Chandon ran at his own expense. One day the Germans refused him entry. Returning home, he donned the full robes and insignia of the Order of Malta, of which he was a member, and reappeared at the hospital, there to be greeted by abject bows and salutes from the German sentries.

Moët et Chandon which, like all champagne firms, has suffered so much from German depredations in the last hundred years, may be said to have taken their revenge in 1902 when their agent in New York, M. George Kessler, brought off a coup which had international repercussions. He somehow succeeded, at the launching in a New York dockyard of the Kaiser's yacht, *Meteor*, in substituting a bottle of Moët for the German *Sekt* which had been provided, and in having Moët in magnums served at the luncheon after the ceremony; this was attended by the American President and Prince Henry of Prussia. The resulting publicity for French champagne so infuriated the Kaiser that he recalled the German Ambassador from Washington.

Since the First World War, Moët et Chandon has broken all records, and now sells ten million bottles a year. This is largely due to the remarkable man who runs it today, Comte Robert de Vogüé. When I first met him, he said without more ado, "My family has been in existence for six centuries, in the male line, and we have never been to Court – not under the Valois or the Bourbons. Nor have we ever had anything to do with politics – certainly not with what passes for politics in France today." This magnificent scorn for politicians is reflected in his haughty features

33

and courteous manner. Nevertheless, this French aristocrat has not found it beneath him to make money in trade. For nearly forty years now, he has been at the head of Moët et Chandon. This is hardly surprising, for wine flows almost as freely as blue blood in the de Vogüé veins. So extensive are their connections with the great vineyards of France (his brother is head of Veuve Clicquot) that – to quote Patrick Forbes again – "A cellar stocked exclusively with wines made by the de Vogües would be of unbeatable quality and range."

Comte Robert de Vogüé's finest moment, historically, came in the Second World War when Champagne was again overrun by the Germans. They commandeered all the champagne, and sales to civilians were forbidden without special authorisation. Some 350,000 bottles were to be despatched each week to the German Armed Forces. As the months passed, these demands increased, and the champagne makers realised that the only hope of saving their stocks consisted in confronting the Germans with a united front and avoiding mutual competition, as in peace-time. In this way in April 1941, thanks to the leadership of Comte Robert-Jean de Vogüé, the *Comté Interprofessionnel du Vin de Champagne* was founded, with its headquarters at Epernay.

Henceforth, the problems were settled between the Germans and the C.I.V.C.; and the individual champagne-maker was relieved of the day-to-day disputes with the Germans. The latter soon realised that this was an ingenious device to counter their demands, which were much more successful when dealing with individuals. In the autumn of 1942, Comte Robert-Jean de Vogüé was ordered to attend a meeting at the German HQ in Rheims. Hardly had it begun, than the Commanding Officer was called to the telephone. When he returned he said to de Vogüé, "I'm sorry. That was the Gestapo on the telephone. You are under arrest for sabotaging our economy." The Comte de Vogüé was imprisoned and sentenced to death for "obstructing German demands". The death sentence was not carried out, although never revoked, and he went through the ordeal of remaining under it in a concentration camp for the rest of the war. It seems that the German authorities, who feared civil unrest in France at a time when every soldier was needed on the

Russian front, deferred the death sentence indefinitely. When de Vogüé was released in 1945 he was awarded the Legion of Honour, and King George VI created him a Member of the Victorian Order.

The imaginative way in which Comte Robert de Vogüé handles public relations is largely responsible for his firm's great success since the war. He told me that he did not believe in wasting money on advertising in the press and on television; he had discovered something much more effective. "We decided," he said, "that our clientele could best be encouraged and enlarged by entertaining them. If the entertainment is lavish enough, they will tell their friends – who will tell their friends – who will tell their friends – and so on.... There can be no better form of publicity...."

His firm accordingly took over the Château de Saran outside Epernay belonging to the Moët family, and turned it into an elaborate guest house. It is furnished in the Louis XVI style, with luxurious double bedrooms, each with its private bathroom, telephone, radio etc. He hires the best chefs and staff in France and employs titled ladies as hostesses. Wine connoisseurs, merchants, writers and journalists from all over the world come annually in their hundreds and stay a few days at Saran, while the best Moët et Chandon vintages flow before, during and after luncheons and dinners consisting of exquisite dishes served by white-gloved, liveried footmen. After half a dozen of these meals, washed down with 1966 Moët et Chandon, it is hardly surprising that a South African journalist who was staying the week-end said to me tipsily, "I'd like to stay in Saran for ever."

The tradition of the "Champagne widows" still flourishes in Moët et Chandon in the person of the charming Comtesse de Maigret who takes an active part in the firm; her husband was a director and she was widowed in 1964. She receives the guests in the Trianon at Epernay, before they go on to Saran. She takes them round the famous chalk cellars in which millions of champagne bottles are housed, revealing an encyclopaedic knowledge of champagne-making and its history since Dom Pérignon's day. She confirmed what I had learned earlier from the Comte de Vogüé, that most of the big champagne firms do not advertise in the conventional way. They prefer to impress the public by welcoming visitors to their cellars – as she had welcomed us – arranging conducted tours for them and filling them up afterwards with champagne. "The cellars of Champagne," she said, "are said to have become the biggest tourist attraction in France, eclipsed in popularity only by the château of Versailles and the Eiffel Tower."

During the past decade a great expansion has taken place in Moët et Chandon due chiefly again to Comte Robert de Vogüé. In 1962 he acquired Ruinart, the oldest of the existing champagne firms; and in 1968 he entered the perfume business, obtaining control of Christian Dior perfumes. In 1970, he took over another champagne firm, Mercier; and in 1971, he merged with Hennessy, the famous Cognac firm.

When I remarked to a senior member of the Ruinart firm (which only retains its title nominally) that this savours of monopoly, he replied, "Well, which is better – to be monopolised by your own countrymen, or by the Americans and Japanese? That's what's happening to many of the big French wine firms now. If we don't amalgamate among ourselves, we'll all be gobbled up by Mr Hiram J. Walker."*

*An American whisky distiller who has bought up a number of French wine firms, including Courvoisier.

4

Bordeaux in the Eighteenth Century –
the Marquis de Segur and Montesquieu

When the traveller drawing near his journey's end first sees
Bordeaux as he descends the green hill of the Bastide, he is
instantly struck by the splendour of the scene unfolding beneath
him: the variegated plain with its countless vineyards; the majestic sweep of the Garonne beyond; the city itself, with the spires
of St André, St Martin and its other antique towers; the semi-
circular port bounded by the great curve of the Chartrons, crowded
with the ships of many nations discharging their cargoes in return
for wine. This together with the vast squares and *allées* built by
Victor Louis and the Gabriels, greatest of French eighteenth-
century architects, forms a city which is peerless in provincial
France.

Bordeaux's prosperity has depended throughout history upon
one commodity. Its chief possession, its first article of commerce,
since Roman times – when the city was called *Bordigala* – down to
our own days, has been the produce of its vines. One square mile
in ten of this landscape is under the grape. The old Gascon saying
is as true today as it was in Plantagenet times: *Le vin de nos
vignes est nôtre substance.*

The eighteenth century was the golden age of Bordeaux when,
as the first port of France, its wines were shipped all over the
world – in return for which from the Antilles, from Martinque,
Guadeloupe and Saint Dominique, it imported coffee, sugar,
indigo, spices, and the rose and cedar woods which were used so
exquisitely, by the great *ébénistes*. Between 1717 and 1789,
Bordeaux's overseas trade increased from 16 million to 250 million
livers. Arthur Young, the English traveller of the 1780's, described

it as "commercially superior even to my native Liverpool"; he praised it for its "busy wine-wharfs, wide boulevards, public parks and flourishing stock market".

This was the century of the great vineyard owners in Bordeaux, some four hundred families, or about two per cent of the population. By the death of Louis XIV in 1712, the *noblesse de l'épée* was on the decline, refusing to consort with the rapidly developing commercial life of the city. A dozen or so scions of the great families remained in Gascony, with names dating back to the wars of the League, or the Hundred Years' War; Albret, Armagnac, de Fumel, Durfort de Duras, the Counts of Preissac, de Citran. But most of them had retired to their châteaux in the Entre-Deux-Mers where, screened behind avenues of plane trees and poplars, they lived in seclusion, seeing no one but themselves, preferring this to sharing the city with the new, commercially active, *noblesse de robe*.* By the end of the seventeenth century the latter, elevated largely by membership of the *Jurade* (the Bordeaux Parliament), had acquired many of the lands and houses of the old nobility. The feudal Albrets and Duras were giving way to the new aristocracy of the Pontacs and Pichons.

Election to the *Jurade* did not in itself confer the patent of nobility. Generally, those elected had worked in some legal capacity for the French Crown, although there were also a number of cases where, "for public service to the *Jurade*", wholesale merchants had acquired titles. According to the eighteenth-century statistician, Nicolai, by 1712, one hundred and seven Parliamentary offices and thirty-four offices at the Cour des Assises bore the title of nobility. The de Pontac family, of present wine renown, date their privileged rank from Arnaud de Pontac, the first President of the *Jurade*, one of the richest men in Bordeaux. The de Tresne family, who later owned the vineyard of Haut-Brion, are descended from a Parliamentary President in the mid-seventeenth century. The name of another President of the *Jurade*, Pichon, is today commemorated in a famous vineyard. Mr Robert Foster, in "The Noble Wine Producers of the Bordelais in the 18th Century", says that seventy-five per cent of the income of these men came

Robe derives from the lawyer's *robe* or uniform.

38

from wine.* So rich were they that "they could maintain both a summer and a winter residence, a retinue of servants, a coach and phaeton, a copious wardrobe and cellar, and collections of silver, china, fine linen and books" – this together with regular theatre and concert *abonnements*, and the occasional trip to the watering places in the Pyrenees.

Although some had become rich through textiles and ceramics, most owed their wealth to the vineyards, in particular to the rapidly developing Médoc peninsula, whose gravelly soil was unsuited to cereals but excellent for the grape, producing the great *crus* of Lafite, Latour, Margaux and Mouton. In normal years, these vineyards yielded anything up to 500 livres an acre; whereas corn or pasture yielded only 50 livres. It is understandable therefore that these hard-headed businessmen preferred to invest their capital in the grape.

Foremost among them in eighteenth-century Bordeaux was the Parliamentary President, Alexandre de Ségur (later Marquis de Ségur), who owned three of the greatest vineyards in the world, Lafite, Latour and Mouton. His fortune evaluated at his death in 1763 of two and a half million pounds included *hôtels* in Paris and Bordeaux, lands in the Ile de France, and the *métairie* of Lhote in the Médoc. Ninety per cent of his income came from the grape, and when he went to Court, Louis XV, remarking that there was no richer subject in his realm, christened him "*Mon Prince de la Vigne*". One day the King commented on the brilliant diamond buttons de Ségur was wearing, saying that the royal treasure possessed nothing as splendid. To which de Ségur replied, "Sire, I am wearing the diamonds from my own vineyard." They were, in fact, flints from the soil of Lafite, perfectly cut and polished.

In the eighteenth century, members of the *Jurade* benefited, as did all the nobility of France, from tax exemptions, including that of the *taille*, (tithe), which the bourgeois and peasants had to pay in full. But this does not appear to have assuaged the appetite of certain vineyard owners. In 1744, the Président de

*His article in The *Economic History Review*, 2nd Series, Vol XI, No: 1, August 1961.

Ségur, submitted an appeal to the Intendant against taxes on his vineyards at Lafite and Latour. According to the Bordeaux *Archives Départementales*, it appears that he falsified his accounts – as did most of his peers – claiming unwarranted relief on meadowland. Earlier, in 1743, a female de Ségur had raised an outcry by claiming that her late father's income had been only 6,000 livres, and that his successors had been over-taxed; whereas, after careful investigation, the fiscal authorities found that he had lived on 100,000 livres a year, and that his coach and horses alone cost 11,000 livres annually.

Among the Ségurs' many properties was one acquired less for its wine production than for the pleasures of its *villégiature* – Francs in the Médoc, embellished with follies, arbours, fishponds and ornamental walks. One of the follies is still standing, the Pavilion of the Twelve Doors. The interior was decorated with divans in crimson velvet, and console tables supporting marble busts of the most important members of the family. Here, one of the greatest receptions of eighteenth-century Bordeaux took place, at the marriage of a Ségur daughter. Each of the hundred guests found at table beneath his napkin a golden *livret des noces* (marriage booklet). The daughter wrote in a letter, "After the wedding, we went to visit the servants and peasants. There was a long table of 100 places for the livery servants, whose variously coloured coats and trimmings looked very picturesque; and another long table for the peasants and workmen. They drank my health with a will. I am very much liked by them, and they have the greatest confidence in me."

Other entertainments on an equally princely scale were given by Maréchal le duc de Richelieu, the victor of Fontenoy. A hundred and fifty guests a night was quite usual in his Bordeaux palace, including the prettiest daughters of the town, regardless of birth. Here, in the company of the leading vineyard owners, the wine flowed. It was thanks largely to the Maréchal de Richelieu that Bordeaux wine replaced burgundy at the French Court. On his arrival as Intendant of Gascony, Richelieu ordered for his table the burgundies to which he was accustomed, Chambertin, Nuits, Pommard, etc. One day he congratulated his *sommelier* on the quite exceptional excellence of the burgundies served at a reception. To his surprise, the *sommelier* informed him that, because the burgundy shipments had been delayed by storms, he had taken the liberty of replacing them surreptitiously by Château Lafite. Richelieu seems to have taken the deception in good part, for from that moment on he never drank anything else. When aged over sixty, he was congratulated by Louis XV on looking twenty years younger than when he had left Paris to become Intendant in Bordeaux. To which Richelieu replied. "Sire, I have discovered the secret of eternal youth – the wine of Château Lafite." After this, the wines of Bordeaux supplanted burgundy at the Court of France, the wits of Paris calling them "*la tisane de Richelieu*" (Richelieu's infusion). The Pompadour took to drinking Lafite, as did her entourage.

Debauches were frequent at the Maréchal's receptions, and he was noted for his gallantries. In the words of the historian, Pariset, Bordeaux had become by the late eighteenth century "a city where luxury vied with immorality, surpassing Paris in opulence and disdain for the value of money, in high prices, audacity and fabulous wealth. In this minor Paris masked balls were frequent, where a thousand persons unknown to one another made assignations."

Among other great eighteenth-century vineyard owners were the de Brassiers, also counsellors to the Bordeaux *Jurade*, who owned, in addition to a city hôtel, three large vineyards, at Moulins, Lamarque and, greatest of all, fabled Beychevelle. The latter was – and still is – architecturally the finest wine château in Gascony, built in the greatest period (1757). It is described in a later act of sale as "a vast château with four wings known as pavilions, whose outhouses consist of coach-houses, granaries, fish-ponds, bowers *chais** and its own cooperage department". The main road from Bordeaux passes the magnificent western façade, while the eastern, with its terraced front, faces the distant Gironde, to which its vineyards and lawns run down.

*These *chais* are sombre halls with enormous beams supported, as if in some Babylonian temple, by a double line of stone columns. Inter-connecting, the *chais* are veritable catacombs, from which the uninitiated would require the clew of Ariadne to find his way back to the light of day.

The Lurs-Saluces family, one of the oldest in Gascony, did not possess property in the Médoc; but they have owned for over two hundred years a château and vineyard in the Sauterne which many connoisseurs regard as superior to all others, Château Yquem. They acquired it in 1785, and still own it today, a château on a small mamelon with twelfth-century turrets. They also owned Le Filhot, finest of the Sauterne châteaux, which they kept until 1936, and de Malle, a seventeenth-century château with a pepper-pot tower and a formal Italian garden. The vineyards of Coutet and Climens also belonged in pre-Revolutionary days to the Lurs-Saluces as did Piada and the Château de Fargues.

If there is not a great deal to be said about these men Brassiers, de Ségur, Lurs-Saluces, etc, as personalities, the same cannot be said of the greatest Frenchman among the eighteenth-century vineyard owners, Montesquieu. His *Lettres Persanes* contain an entire letter about wine and viniculture. Through his father, he inherited the vines of Martillac, Olivier and Léognan in the Graves; through his mother, La Brède (by whose name he is best known, the Baron de la Brède). From an uncle he inherited the vines of Montesquieu in Lavardac; and his wife brought him with her dowry Clairac and Lartigue. These considerable estates did not however produce wine of the first quality, and his annual income always seems to have been uncertain. Although he regarded himself as a competent businessman much concerned with the sale of his wine, he was an intellectual and did not possess what we would call "the real estate" talent of the Ségurs and Brassiers. On 1 January 1727 he wrote to a friend, "I have sold my wine so badly this year that I can't afford to go to Paris;" and a number of his books such as *Le Temple de Cnide* were written as pot-boilers to support his vineyards. In *Histoires Véritables* he wrote. "I'm trying to write a book which will *sell* – I don't mind if it's good, bad or indifferent provided it helps reestablish my vineyards after this disastrous year."

Well aware of the publicity value of the written word, he once said he was not sure whether he sold wine to write books, or wrote books to sell wine. To one of his English clients he wrote, "The success that my books have had in your country has contributed, it appears, to the success of my wine." This practical or commercial approach, unusual in an intellectual, had a considerable influence on the political and philosophical writings by which he is best known. It is also in keeping with his admiration for the practical English, as expressed in his *Esprit des Lois*.

His Château de la Brède, although surrounded by a park with grazing cattle and fine lawns *à l'Anglaise*, still exhales with its moated walls something of the mediaeval atmosphere. His greatest pleasure, he used to say, was to furnish it in the English manner. "It is in truth a Gothic castle," he wrote, "its interior is embellished with the charming decoration inspired by my stay in England."

Montesquieu ran into serious trouble with the royal Intendant, Boucher, over his vineyards. Boucher considered that the habit among Gascon landowners of preferring to cultivate the grape instead of cereals endangered the province's food supply. In 1724 he issued an edict that many of the vineyards in the Entre-Deux-Mers were to be uprooted and the land sown with other crops. This provoked the vine owners, of whom the most articulate, if not the most powerful, was Montesquieu. He protested that if this instruction were followed in Gascony, other parts of France would plant vines extensively and take possession of their valuable wine market. Foreigners like the Portuguese, he said, would follow suit, producing wine *à la manière Bordelaise*. To the authorities he wrote, "Foreigners drink more wine than formerly, and prefer the great variety of our Gascon wines. Gascony is particularly suited to this form of cultivation.... In any case, the proprietors surely know better what to do with their own lands than does a Minister or an Intendant."

The Intendant Boucher was annoyed by the writer's accusation of ignorance. In retaliation, he accused Montesquieu of hypocrisy, because vineyards covered most of the philosopher's domains; he pointed out that Montesquieu's was a short-sighted view, for the excessive cultivation of the grape would finally lower the price of wine. The argument rumbled on for years until, under mounting pressure from Montesquieu and his peers, the Intendant withdrew the Edict. It was some measure of the power of the Bordelais wine interests, even when confronted by the Crown of France.

In the latter half of the eighteenth century, the big land-owners increased their vineyard acreage immensely as the smaller tenant growers, the *métayers*, were forced to sell. In one parish, Villeneuve d'Ornon, seventy small owners had only 75 acres of vines between them, whereas three big land-owners had 850 acres. As these "Princes of the Grape" gradually established their monopoly, they bitterly opposed a municipal plan to run a road from Bordeaux through the Médoc, to the most northerly point with its port. The Bordeaux municipality and merchants who marketed the proprietors' wine contended that this would facilitate the sea transport of wine, because it could be shipped at the point of the Médoc, thereby avoiding the long voyage up the Gironde estuary with its dangerous shoals and currents. But the big proprietors feared that a road would bring the Bordeaux merchants into contact with the small wine-growers on the route, with whom they would do business direct. They therefore used their influence to have the proposal vetoed.

At this time, only the "Bourgeois de Bordeaux" – which included all the big proprietors – had the privilege of selling their wine tax-free in the city, and they alone controlled the retail market. A peasant working on the *métayage* system on a great wine estate (that is, possessing a small part of its wine), could not enter Bordeaux to sell it. In the *Archives Départementales* is a significant comment by a contemporary tax official: "The peasants on the *métayage* wine estates may be contrasted with those working on arable land. In the latter case, both landlord and peasant sell the same wheat at the same price. But in the vineyards, the peasant *métayers* sell their wine at a quarter of the price obtained by the proprietor."

As these peasant *métayers* had little contact with the "Bourgeois de Bordeaux", and being without enough capital to postpone their sales until the best buyer could be found, they generally had to sell to the proprietor himself. The English traveller, Arthur Young, pointed out pertinently that at the end of the eighteenth century vintners who could afford to retain their wine made much greater profits because, "maturing adds considerably to the value of the wine . . . the most successful are those who have the greatest capital, men who not only possess many acres of their own vines, but who buy up the wine of their smaller neighbours." Moreover, the small men did not generally have the capital to buy the vats, casks and presses required to produce good wine; they had to depend for these services on the owners.

Towards the end of the eighteenth century, the big owners were buying up the properties of the small men at such a rate that in 1781 (eight years before the Revolution), the inhabitants of the village of Espesson protested in writing to the civic authorities that, "Most of the land is now passing out of the hands of the *taille*-payer into those of the privileged class, which has eliminated many small farms in order to plant vines." Again, at Laborde-en-Médoc the peasants complained that in order to buy bread for their families, they were being forced to sell their vineyard holdings.

Another form of virtually forced sale by the peasants was caused by the landlord allowing them to accumulate arrears or debts over a period as long as twenty years, and then demanding a huge lump sum. The peasant, being unable to pay, had to sell his holding. In 1726, the Président de Ségur brought a lawsuit against a peasant for twenty-nine years' arrears of rent. The Marquis de Donissan did the same against the peasants of Pelit in 1756. Nor did these *noblesse de robe* confine their land accumulation to that of peasant proprietors; they were equally ready to purchase land belonging to their "betters", the impoverished *noblesse de l'épée*, in particular from the widows of those ancient families.

All this may seem very heinous in our egalitarian age, but *autre temps autres moeurs*, and such behaviour was fairly common throughout Europe in the eighteenth century. It also conferred very considerable benefits on society. Thanks to this accumulation of vast wealth, the *noblesse de robe* had become a highly cultivated class. The eighteenth century in Bordeaux was, as elsewhere in Europe, an age of great elegance and taste unsurpassed before or since – when its finest buildings were erected, when furniture and ceramics were works of art, when manners were most polished, and most libertine.

The wealth of these wine families enabled them to play a great part in the embellishment of the city at this, the most propitious moment for the erection of monuments. Bordeaux is still the most beautiful city in provincial France. A century before Baron Haussman opened up the great boulevards of Paris, these families had endowed Bordeaux with the broad streets, the great public parks and squares which we walk in today, and with Victor Louis's opera house, the finest in the world. "Never," wrote Arthur Young in 1787, "did I behold anything that can compare with the great theatre of Bordeaux." Its façade is a Corinthian colonnade of twelve pillars, of Parthenon proportions, each four feet in diameter and surmounted by statues, nine of them representing the Muses, and three the Goddesses.

Among other buildings by Victor Louis is the great unfinished Château du Bouillh in the Cubzanais belonging to the la Tour du Pin family (another big vineyard owner). It had been intended as a welcome for Louis XVI on his first official visit to Bordeaux, planned for 1790, and it was to have rivalled Versailles. The Revolution came before it could be completed; the hemicycle and the chapel with pediment, all that remains, give some idea of the grandious plan. For the Marquis de Lurs-Saluces of Château Yquem fame, Louis also created the famous music-room in the Marquis's town house. At this time, too, the great Parisian architects, the Gabriels, father and son, came to Bordeaux, attracted by its wealth and remuneration, to build the Bourse and the Place Royale, both buildings unsurpassed in eighteenth-century Europe.

In the late eighteenth century, too, Bordeaux porcelain reached its apogee; and the rich wine families ordered their own private services, the decoration revolving around their coats-of-arms. The great Intendant Boucher possessed a magnificent service, as did the Dauphin who ordered one for his wedding. Services are still to be seen today made for the Ségur, de Sourdis and de Gasq families.

When the Revolution broke out, the Jacobin pro-Consuls Tallien and Ysabeau arrived in Bordeaux dragging the guillotine behind them. They were, it may well be surmised, not particularly well-disposed towards vineyard owners. The Marquis de Ségur managed to emigrate in time, but such was his ill-repute that his successor at Lafite, the Président de Pichard – to whom he had sold the vineyard for a million livres – was guillotined. About a dozen of the owners were executed, the rest fled and their vineyards were sequestrated as national property. M. de Lavessier, an uncle of the Lurs-Saluces family, had represented wine interests in the Parliament of Bordeaux for decades. He was condemned to death and, during the execution, his wife was placed in a pillory facing the guillotine, with her two sons bound hand and foot beside her.

Another vineyard owner, M. Dudon, who had been Procureur and Avocat-Général to the *Jurade*, was arrested with his son, and both were sentenced to death. Madame Dudon, the son's wife, confident in her powers of persuasion and beauty, threw herself at the feet of the sinister pro-Consul Ysabeau, and begged that her husband should be reprieved. Ysabeau said he would spare him if such a rich vineyard owner could immediately produce 25,000 gold francs. It was not easy at this time to collect so large a sum; the Republic had not minted any gold, and had forbidden people under pain of death to hoard it. In despair, Madame Dudon rushed to all her friends and acquaintances, finally managing to collect the required sum, with which she returned to Ysabeau. He accepted it saying, to her relief, that her husband had already left prison that night. But it was a cruel mockery; her husband had indeed left prison that night, but on his way to the guillotine.

Among other vineyard owners who perished on the scaffold was the Comte d'Hargicourt, owner of Château Margaux, together with his wife, the daughter of another vineyard owner, the Marquis de Fumel. The Marquis de la Tour du Pin owned the beautiful Château du Bouillh (designed by Louis, as already described), with its famous vineyard. According to his daughter-in-law, the celebrated memorialist, Henriette de la Tour du Pin, he was scrupulously attentive to his duties as landlord, and devoted much time to running his wine estate. After Louis XVI's enforced visit to Paris at the behest of the Convention, he was unwise enough to accept from the King the post of Minister of War. He was thus in command at Versailles when the monarch set off on the ignominious journey, with the heads of his murdered guards mounted on pikes in front of his carriage. The Marquis was tried and guillotined, and an order was made for the arrest of his son and daughter-in-law at Le Bouillh, and for his property and vineyards to be sequestrated. Representatives of the People appeared without warning at Le Bouillh and affixed seals on every room. His son and daughter-in-law had escaped just in time, he to Mirambeau, she to Bordeaux where, disguised as a "grisette" she witnessed the horrible scenes of which she has left such a graphic description.

She would almost certainly have perished too had she not been befriended by Mme de Fontenay, the mistress of the revolutionary pro-Consul Tallien. This remarkable woman, the daughter of a Spanish banker named Cabarrus, had before the Revolution married the Marquis de Fontenay. When he died in 1790, she went to live with Tallien, with whom she used her influence to save many people in Bordeaux from the guillotine. Thanks to her, Mme de la Tour du Pin was able to leave by boat with her family for America, not returning to Le Bouillh until after 1796, when better conditions under the Directoire had been established, and the sequestration order had been rescinded. But the famous vineyard was now worth very little. "The war with England," she wrote, "has brought the price of wine down to rock-bottom ... my husband has installed a distillery, but the profits from this innovation barely cover our living expenses."

Such was the Revolution in Bordeaux. The tables were brutally turned on the Ségurs and their peers, the prisons filled with the richest owners and wine merchants, ransomed and re-imprisoned according to the caprice and cupidity of the pro-Consuls. In front of the wine establishments on the Quai des Chartons, brigands in red caps celebrated the apotheosis of the sanguinary Marat in the best wines of the Médoc.

5

The Wine *Négociants*

Already, in the late seventeenth century, a new type of "Prince of the Grape" was appearing on the French scene, the *négociant*. In the new business world which was developing, the *robe* aristocracy in France was, as we have seen, not ashamed to make money out of wine. As overseas sales increased, they began to feel the need for a middle-man to negotiate the sales with their expanding clientele. Hence the *négociant*. Generally these men were not French, but came from countries with which France had a flourishing wine trade, England, Ireland, Scotland, the Low Countries. Their surnames reveal their national origins – Barton, Johnston, Skinner, Lawton, Schÿler, most of whose descendants are still directing wine firms with those names today.

At the outset they were regarded as not quite gentlemen, although some of them, such as Hugh Barton, came from Irish county families. A gentleman was still not supposed to dabble in commerce, although an exception was made to a certain extent in the wine trade, because the *négociant* would presumably be dealing with gentlemen, and he would know how to behave. Nevertheless in Bordeaux, they were virtually ostracised from the main body of the town, having to reside in the marshy and insalubrious area to the north known as the Faubourg des Chartrons. It is still today the centre of the *négociants* wineries, a place of dark and narrow alleys and hidden turnings, giving onto the *chais* or overground cellars, where the great vats are stored in their thousands.

In the late seventeenth century, the Faubourg des Chartrons formed a small colony on its own, separated from Bordeaux by the forbidding fortress of Trompeyte (which Charles VI had built to keep his unruly Gascon subjects in order). In the evening, its military barriers were lowered, and a long detour around it had to be made to reach the town proper, whose gates were closed at 11 pm. Thus these *négociants* became a race apart. Protestants nearly all of them, with their own church in the Faubourg des Chartrons, they lived from the sale of the grape, and became unified in the course of the next two centuries by economic, religious and family ties.

The history of the Barton family is typical of these early *négociants*. Thomas Barton, of an Anglo-Irish Protestant family, came to Bordeaux in 1723 to trade in contraband wool. According to Mr Cyril Ray in his excellent account of the Bartons, *Fide et Fortitudine*, Irish wool then commanded the highest price in Europe, on account of its superior quality. For this reason the British government, to protect their own sheep-farmers, forbade its export to the Continent. The price which the French were willing to pay was three or four times higher than in England – putting a premium on smuggling wool which no human nature, let alone Irish human nature, could resist. Their vessels which brought the wool returned laden with claret and brandy for the English, at correspondingly advantageous prices. In England, neither peer nor squire was averse to avoiding duty on his Bordeaux or Cognac, when he could have his cellars filled for half the price, provided he asked no unnecessary questions about its provenance.

By the mid-eighteenth century, Thomas Barton and his son had abandoned wool-smuggling for wine – in the opposite direction, to England – which proved even more lucrative. As yet they owned no vineyards. They either negotiated contracts for the proprietor, or bought the wine from him themselves and adapted it to the taste of their clientele in England. They became highly skilled in "blending", that is, mixing Bordeaux with other wines such as Spanish Beni Carlo, or inferior native wines from the Côte du Rhône – practices which are forbidden today. In a municipal raid on the Chartrons in 1765, adulterated wine of this kind was found in a *négociant's* cellar; and a law was passed by the Bordeaux *Jurade* prohibiting *coupage* (blending) on pain of confiscation of the wine and loss of trading rights. Barton, on behalf of the English *négociants*, objected strongly to this law, on the ground that his customers in England preferred blended wines. If the blending, he contended, was not undertaken in Bordeaux, it would be in England, with a corresponding loss of revenue for Bordeaux. The hard-headed Bordeaux Parliamentarians appear to have seen the logic of this, and the law was rescinded.

This "blending", while perfectly legitimate if done to improve the quality of the wine, can easily become a euphemism for "adulterating". An unscrupulous *négociant*, aware that his overseas clients do not possess discerning palates, can (or *could* until the law of 1922) defraud them in this way. Even the Parisians – so the Bordelais claim – can be hoodwinked into drinking a pseudo Saint Julien, a false Saint Estèphe, or the Cantenacs and Pauillacs which are entirely without civic status. In those days, the dishonest *négociant* would go quite openly to the Aude or the Hérault with his barrels, which he would fill from the local hogsheads; he would then infuse in them for twenty-four hours a packet of orris root, to give the authentic Médoc flavour. On other occasions, he had recourse to "chemists" who invented aromatic saps with which the most humble *vin ordinaire* could be given the flavour of a Médoc or a Sauterne.

In the course of time the *négociant*, who had originally acted for the vineyard proprietor, became a middle-man buying the wine in bulk from the proprietor, and then selling it on his own to overseas clients. Proprietors like the Marquis de Ségur generally left the bartering with the *négociants* to their bailiffs. In the mid-eighteenth century, we find the Ségur's bailiff at Château Latour, M. Lamothe, giving some idea of the tough bargaining skill of the *négociants*, describing them as "Matadors", referring to them as "those inexorable Irish *négociants*. The rocks of Cardouan,"* he says, "are less dangerous to the wine ships than are the *négociants* to the vineyard owners" – which shows at least that the great proprietors did not have it all their own way.

Towards the end of the century, the Bartons had expanded into actual ownership of the vineyards, buying the Château de Bosq

*A dangerous shoal in the estuary of the Gironde.

C

with its vineyards in the Médoc. This was a departure from tradition, for the *négociants* had always avoided commitments with
property; but the Bartons pointed the way to what was to become
normal practice in the nineteenth and twentieth centuries. In spite
of this, although now completely domiciled in Bordeaux, whence
came all their wealth, the Bartons never regarded themselves as
French. As if to insist on their Irishness, Thomas Barton bought
the Grove estate in County Tipperary for £30,000. Some of his
grandchildren, profiting from his fortune, carved out distinguished
careers for themselves in England and Ireland; one became an
MP, two became generals; one Barton girl married a peer, another
a baronet. Even today the head of the family in Bordeaux, Ronald
Barton, talks French with an English accent.

By the end of the eighteenth century the insalubrious Chartrons
district had been transformed, the marshes drained and buildings
almost worthy of the rest of Bordeaux erected. The more prominent
négociants were now living very comfortably on the Pavé des
Chartrons, in elegant mansions built at the best period of French
architecture. The vaulted vestibules, broad staircases, large salons
with marquetry and sculptured panelling, attest to their affluence.
Arthur Young in his *Travels in France* just before the Revolution
was shocked that some of them were "keeping mistresses as
expensive as those in Paris"; that "the Bordeaux *négociants* keep
dancing girls and eat huge banquets off silver plate." While
François Mauriac, the modern novelist of the Bordelais, says of
them more sardonically, "This shows how wine ennobles. By the
end of the eighteenth century, they had become the *aristocratie
commerciale*. If a *courtier* [wine-broker] does not quite attain to
the nobility of a *négociant*, he is at least one up socially on the
liberal professions – and streets ahead of the bureaucratic rabble."

Mutatis mutandis, the Barton family history applies to most of
the Anglo-Irish families on the Quai des Chartrons, the Johnstons,
Lawtons, Lynchs, etc. The Johnstons for instance, of Scots origin,
had settled in Bordeaux in 1729, where they founded an export-
import firm trading at first in coffee, cotton, sugar, incense, whale
oil, liquorice and walnuts. They soon went into wine; and when
trade with England was interrupted by the Napoleonic wars, they

ingeniously transferred their business to the United States. By 1810, they had over a thousand American clients for their Bordeaux wines.

During the Revolution, the *négociants* were generally regarded by the Revolutionaries as members of the *ancien régime*, if only on account of their wealth. Among those arrested was Hugh Barton, who appears to have been destined for the guillotine. He was released thanks to his aunt, whose pregnancy seems to have touched the rough hearts of the revolutionaries. He then made his way to Ireland, but not before – according to the family legend – he had set fire to the guillotine. The fire was extinguished, but his act delayed executions for several days and – who knows – gained time for reprieves.

In order to protect his wine property which he, as an enemy alien, was not allowed to retain, Hugh Barton cleverly arranged that it should be managed in Bordeaux by a fellow *négociant*, Daniel Guestier, in the latter's name. Barton, for his part, undertook to manage Guestier's wine interests in England. The difficulty of carrying on business under war conditions, and at such a distance, was very great. Nevertheless, with perfect trust and confidence in each other, these two men contrived to continue during the Napoleonic wars, each in their own names and respective countries, as if they were independent. Not until the First Empire was a formal act of partnership entered into, and the present well-known firm of *Barton et Guestier* was born.*

The Revolution and the Napoleonic wars, in which England blockaded the French Atlantic ports, brought the wine trade in Bordeaux to a standstill. But the efforts of Napoleon's votaries to stir up hatred in the city against the Anglo-Irish *négociants* failed completely. To the Bordelais, the Englishman had always been a creator of his wealth, and his principal client. He realised that the foreign *négociants* were as necessary to his well-being as

---

*A curious example of history repeating itself in this firm occurred in the Second World War. Under the German occupation of 1940-45, the present head of the firm, Ronald Barton, who had British nationality, had to flee the country, leaving his affairs again in Guestier hands. He joined the British Army, in which he had a distinguished career, acting at one point as liaison officer with the Free French. In 1945 he returned and took over his firm again.

the grapes of his soil. Washington Irving, travelling in Gascony at this time wrote, "The emptiness of the roads, the piling up of wine vats without destination, the ever diminishing prices obtained for them, make people realise that the English, by withdrawing owing to the war, have created their desert and their ruin."

It is not surprising therefore that when the English army under Lord Charles Beresford appeared before the gates of Bordeaux in March 1814, it received a tumultuous reception. The Mayor of Bordeaux who welcomed Lord Charles was the Irish wine *négociant*, John Lynch, of the firm of that name. For his services to Napoleon he had been created a Count of the Empire; but this did not prevent him offering Lord Charles the keys of the city, tearing off his tricolour sash of office, and replacing it with a white one. He climbed to the top of St Michael's tower and cried from it, "*Vive les Bourbons!*" Unfortunately for him, at this point, Napoleon returned from Elba and the Hundred Days began. Lynch beat a hurried retreat to Ireland, from which he returned only when Louis XVIII was safely installed on the throne. For this the grateful monarch later created him a peer of France. As we have seen on several occasions before in the wine trade, to these hard-headed merchants "business is always business", and there is nothing shameful about being a Vicar of Bray.

The nineteenth century was the great age of the *négociants*. The Comte de Tournon, the famous Prefect of Bordeaux under Louis XVIII, fully appreciating the changed social and economic conditions after the Revolution, promoted businessmen and merchants to the highest administrative posts throughout the province. He encouraged the wine *négociants*, Daniel Guestier and William Johnston, to found the Banque de Bordeaux for financing overseas investments. In conjunction with the great ship-owner, Balguerie-Stuttenberg,* Daniel Guestier also founded a company for

---

*His father Stuttenberg from Lübeck was a wine *négociant* who introduced into Bordeaux the modern capitalist methods he had learnt in England.

building the magnificent bridge which still spans the Garonne in Bordeaux. It cost 6½ million francs, of which the Bordelais merchants furnished one third, the rest being contributed by the State.

These men now ruled Bordeaux. Under the Orléans monarchy their commercial aristocracy came into its full prime – the reign, it was said, of the *sublimes épiciers*. Many of them, following the earlier example of the Bartons, bought up the great vineyards, in disarray after the Revolution. The Guestier family bought Beychevelle in 1825, and the Scots Johnstons bought Lescure in 1841 – described in the sale as *le domaine le plus fastueux de tout*. The Johnstons also acquired the vineyards of Dauzac, La Maqueline and Ducru-Beaucaillon, the last being sold to the wife of Nathaniel Johnston for one million francs. The Johnstons, incidentally, are unusual among the foreign *négociants* in that they became French and, after renouncing their Protestant faith, Catholic. Although their origins are as impeccably Anglo-Saxon as the Bartons, it is noticeable even today on entering their homes or offices that the atmosphere is reminiscent of pre-war France; whereas the Barton establishments are as cold and formal as the London offices of Saccone and Speed.

By the 1850s the Johnston family was living on the Pavé des Chartrons in great style, with a teeming family, nine of them attended by fifteen servants. One of the Johnston daughters married P. F. Guestier, and they lived at 39 Pavé des Chartrons with two sons and three daughters. In addition to a tutor and a music-teacher, they employed three *valets de chambre*, three housemaids, a chef and chef's assistant, a maid-of-all-work, and a coachman whose wife acted as concierge. Washington Irving stayed with the Johnstons at this time, and tells how "on hunting days we rose at 5 am to be off to the Médoc to hunt the hare with the Barton pack".

What is today the biggest wine *négociant* firm in Bordeaux Cruze et Cie, was founded in the late Napoleonic period by another foreigner. In 1810 Hermann Cruze, the youngest son of a Holstein clergyman, emigrated to Bordeaux with very little capital.

Through sheer hard work he had by 1819 founded his own firm, and soon had a monopoly of the wine trade with Germany and Denmark. Today, Cruze et Cie own five of the most famous châteaux in the Médoc, together with their wine growths – Issan, Pontet-Canet, Laujac, Le Taillan and La Dame Blanche, the first being the oldest *château-fort* in the Médoc. Thus a Danish wine *négociant* now owns one of the most feudal castles in France.*

A similar tale of successful post-Revolution *négociant* foundation is that of the Luzes who, in the early nineteenth century ingeniously used their many consular appointments all over the world to promote their wine sales. Of Teutonic origin the founder, Alfred Luze, was Consul-General to the Grand Duke of Hesse. In 1820, he founded his wine firm in Bordeaux, dealing largely with foreign markets in northern Europe. Meanwhile his brother had become Consul-General for Switzerland in New York; his son became Consul of Bavaria and another son, through acquaintance with Metternich, the Austrian Consul. This quartet of diplomatic posts was of the greatest value in selling the Luze wines to the crowned heads of Europe. Today the four directors of the firm each owns a château in the Médoc; and one of them, the Comte Bertrand du Vivier also owns the famous stud-farm at Mallaret.

Another well-known family of *négociants* dating from about the same period are the Calvets. They are unusual in that they are French; a member of the family commented almost wistfully to me, "It really is odd that we have done so well in Bordeaux, considering that we are not foreigners." They came to Bordeaux during the Revolution from the Rhône where their founder, a

*For this very reason Chateau Issan deserves a word of description, as well as for its chequered history. In the early Middle Ages, it was known as Château Théoban, and belonged successively to the baronnies of Noalhan, Mayrac, Salignac and Ecodera de Boysse, and finally to the Issanault family, from which it now takes its name. When the English were ejected from Gascony in 1453, their last stand was at Issan. Having occupied it for several years, the soldiers had acquired a taste for its wine; when they left they took the entire contents of the cellar with them, hundreds of vats of wine, to remind the English barons in their gloomy fortresses on the Welsh and Scots borders of the sunny lands they had once owned. Its wine has ever since been sold largely on the English market, and is perhaps the best known Bordeaux in our country. The Comte de Foix who defeated the English in 1453 received Issan as a reward, and it remained in the Foix family for several centuries.

doctor, had espoused the Royalist cause. Although they are today one of the first wine families in Bordeaux, they have steadfastly refused to own their own wine châteaux – as most of the other *négociants* now do – preferring to remain as middle-men in the old eighteenth-century tradition.

Most of the wine magnates of Bordeaux have interests other than wine. The most popular is the turf. It is notable, incidentally, how the possession of great wealth through wine has, for over a century in France, gone with a predilection for the race-course. Just as in our country it is said that no brewer has truly "arrived" socially, whatever his wealth, until he owns a grouse-moor, so in nineteenth-century France no rich Bordeaux wine merchant could enter *le monde* except through the stable-door.

Today the most famous stud of Bordeaux is at Mallaret in the Médoc. It is owned and run by the Comte Bertrand du Vivier, chairman of the wine *négociants*, Luze et Cie. This tall, distinguished-looking man took me round his stud and told me more about the habits and eccentricities of his stallions than about his grapes. Horses bred at Mallaret have won most of the big French races, the Prix de Diane, the Derby du Midi, and so on. He also runs a pack of hounds.

When at lunch in his eighteenth-century château, I complimented him on the magnificent wine he offered me, he told me that it was indeed one of his best wines, but that he was appalled at the price he was having to charge for it. I was surprised that a wine merchant should deplore obtaining high prices for his produce. "No, it doesn't follow," he said. "The market has expanded so much since the war due to American and Japanese clients that demand has outrun supply. This puts the prices up. This in the long run is not a good thing for us. We find ourselves, by the laws of economics, forced to supply this foreign market at the expense of our own home market – which is the reliable one. When an international crisis or a war comes, the foreign market collapses, and we have lost many of our French clients."

I felt I had learned something about economics, particularly as the two other guests at the lunch table were Americans. They were staying with him, on the friendliest, most intimate terms. I later discovered that they were making a film of Bordeaux wine production, which would be shown all over the United States. The vineyard and cellars they had chosen to film were Mallaret.

The other great wine name connected with the turf in Bordeaux is Guestier (of the firm of Barton-Guestier). In 1873, the Guestiers founded a racing stable which in one year alone had 140 winners, mostly in Paris and Deauville. They have been intimately connected with the turf for five generations; between 1875 and 1944, some 900 horses raced under Guestier colours. The same can be said for the Fould family, bankers who own the finest wine château in the Médoc, Beychevelle. One of them was the founder of the *Société d'Encouragement des Courses*, which become the exclusive Jockey Club; he was regarded as the first gentleman-jockey in France.

6

The Rothschilds in Bordeaux

In the mid-nineteenth century the vineyards of Bordeaux were struck by the deadly disease Odium – with such force that within a year production was halved. Remedial measures were discovered, but their application proved so expensive that many of the smaller owners could not afford them. It was now that the big business-men of Paris, the bankers and financiers, moved in. They took a risk, but they acquired high quality vineyards at a low price. When they had succeeded, with their considerable resources, in mastering the disease, they possessed some of the most lucrative soil in Europe. It was then that the names of the great Second Empire bankers appeared on the Bordeaux scene – Péreire, Fould, Michel, Heine, the stockbroker Comyet and, greatest of all, Rothschild. In 1835 Baron Nathaniel Rothschild, of the English branch, acquired Mouton; and his kinsman, Baron James de Rothschild, bought Lafite in 1868.

Bertal in his anecdotal book *La Vigne – Voyage autour des Vins de France* describes how, when visiting the Médoc in the mid-nineteenth century at vintage time, he became aware of this "Banker atmosphere of Bordeaux"; how he was passed on the road by fine carriages whose occupants made him feel he was back in the counting-houses of Paris. "Here," he writes, "come the Péreires in their elegant phaeton, then the Vicomtesse Aguado, the Halphen ladies, the d'Erlangers.... Ah, the Rothschilds! When I was at Lafite and the pretty young Baronne de Rothschild walked through the vineyard under her parasol, one of the old women working on the vines said to me, 'Ah, to be a Rothschild, to possess so many millions – *and* Château Lafite! To be so beautiful, so young, with such pretty children! With a husband who loves you, and is a Rothschild! A husband who is also good, kind and gracious! Frankly, that is too much for one woman! No, no, it is unfair... !' "

First place among the contemporary "Princes of the Grape" must go to Baron Philippe de Rothschild who owns Mouton, the great-grandson of Nathaniel Rothschild who bought it in 1853. When I stayed with him in 1972, he explained something of the extraordinary "wine explosion" which has occurred since the war, how vast new markets have opened all over the world, particularly in America, how the whole wine market has been transformed since 1945. "Between the Allegheny mountains and the Pacific," he said, "tens of thousands of American families now appreciate and drink first-class French wine – who did not before."

A rugged, warm-natured and outspoken man, he admits that although he is a Rothschild, with all that the name denotes, he still likes making money; and he is now concentrating on this new American market. "But to get into it," he said, "has not been easy. For forty years, you see, while I have owned Mouton, I have laboured under having my wine in the second category."

I wondered how the great wine of Mouton could conceivably be in any *second* category, and how in any case this could hamper the sale of such nectar today. He explained.

"The wine classification which put us in the second category," he said, "was made as long ago as 1855. So conservative are the Bordeaux vintners, it has never changed since. You see, our wine world here, is full of little parochial jealousies. Thanks to that 1855 classification, many châteaux wines still enjoy a high category today, which they don't deserve. They know that in a fresh classification they would be relegated."

"But surely," I said, "what does it matter? Everyone knows that Mouton is one of the great wines of the world – quite as good as any of the wines in the first category?"*

"No," he replied. "I told you about the huge new market in the American Middle West. Of course, people on the eastern sea-

*There are five wines in the First Category – Lafite, Latour, Maraux, Haut-Brion, Yquem.

board of the United States, New York, Washington and so on, know that my wine is first-class. But these new millionaires in the Middle West don't. When they give a dinner party, they want to be able to tell their guests that their wine is 'the Tops' – just as the pictures on their walls are genuine Picassos. It wouldn't do to have anything second-class, or you lose face. And that's where the money is, I tell you – between the Allegheny mountains and the Pacific ocean."

Philippe de Rothschild lives in state at Mouton for most of the year, entertaining the many guests who stay with him to epicurean meals in a different room each day. He has a special guest house for them, Petit Mouton, luxuriously appointed in Second Empire style, all the rooms interconnected by a telephone service as in a hotel. He likes to do his business from his bed, and throughout the morning he sends out a series of orders to his staff, as well as having long conversations with his guests over the Mouton intercom. I once interviewed him in bed where, clad in white silk pyjamas, with his labrador beside him, he regularly interrupted the conversation to ring up Paris or New York.

His well-paid *vignerons* respect his encyclopaedic knowledge of wine-making, acquired in fifty years of ownership of Mouton, since he inherited it from his father in 1922. His *Maître des Chais*, M. Raoul, has an almost religious veneration for him. "You see," M. Raoul told me as he showed me round the cellars, "M. le Baron is not like most of the big vineyard owners here. They leave the work to their Factors. But M. le Baron, he supervises everything himself. And he seizes on the smallest mistake. Very frightening he can be. But it's best that way. Because he's fair."

M. Raoul has been showing visitors round the cellars with their thousands of cobweb-covered bottles for over forty years, and he never seems to tire of it. He remained here throughout the Second World War in the absence of his master, looking after his interests and protecting them from the Germans. Not only does he reign undisputed today over the *chais* but, such is his love of being with his bottles, he insists on uncorking and serving them at his master's table for the gastronome lunch and dinner parties given for the fortunate guests.

When Philippe de Rothschild inherited Mouton, he found it in a state of some dilapidation. His father, although a rich man, appears to have taken little interest in it because of the post-war slump. Philippe de Rothschild immediately set to work to exploit its potentialities. He erected new buildings and modernised the old; he introduced modern methods of management and book-keeping; he employed ingenious publicity methods, such as commissioning each year a well-known artist to design his bottle labels – Marie Laurencin, Cocteau, Braque, Dali, Moore, etc. But his greatest publicity achievement since the war is his unique Wine Museum, which has brought thousands of visitors from all over the world to Mouton. He and his artistically talented wife, Pauline, took many years to form the collection, which was opened in 1962. His Wine Museum covers the entire field of wine icnography from Mycenean times to those of Picasso. Among the thousand exhibits, I particularly admired the sixteenth-century Strasbourg and Nederweiler tapestries, five of them, each ten feet square; they are the only tapestries depicting the various stages of wine production I have ever seen – magnificent bucolic scenes reminiscent of the *Très Riches Heures du Duc de Berry*. Most of the exhibits are antique, from all over the world – wine ewers of the Moghul princes from Agra, and Chinese drinking vessels, as well as French ceramics of the eighteenth century. There are one or two moderns, a Rouault of "The Drunkard", and the bizarre abstract work of a contemporary American sculptor, Richard Lippold, entitled the "Spirit Vine", a tracery of gold thread and platinum.

During the Second World War, Mouton and its owner suffered the fate of all occupied France. Baron Philippe was arrested on racial grounds by the Vichy government and put in prison; here he organised amenities for his fellow prisoners, language courses and PT classes. He escaped in 1941 and crossed the Pyrenees on foot in the company of a band of smugglers, making his way through Lisbon to London, where he joined the Free French; he finished the war as head of the civil administration of Le Havre, with a Croix de Guerre and the Legion of Honour. By a freak of fortune, his cellars with hundreds of thousands of pounds' worth of wine were not stolen or sold off cheap by the Germans, because Mouton had been earmarked for the Nazi leader, Hermann Göring, as "confiscated Jewish property". It was therefore to remain inviolate until after the war, for Göring was too busy at the time with his *Luftwaffe*; he said the wine would keep until after victory. But victory when it came was not German, and the Liberation in 1944 was so swift that the retreating Germans had no time to carry away their Air Marshal's vinous loot.

Baron Philippe told me that after the Second World War a movement was started in Bordeaux to end the internecine rivalry between the wine firms, all jealous of one another's place in the 1855 classification. "It required the war," he said, "with its privations and the presence of an occupying power controlling our wine commerce to bring this about. At first, the idea was considered Utopian. How, it was asked, could centuries of bickering be eliminated? But in 1944 the *Comité Interprofessionnel du Vin de Bordeaux* was founded. It purchased a house in Bordeaux where all wine merchants could feel at home and rub shoulders with their business competitors."

That he practises what he preaches was clear from his appreciative remarks about one of his great rivals, Château Yquem. "The Marquis de Lurs-Saluces did most for the *Comité Interprofessionnel*," he said. "When he returned in 1945 from a prisoner-of-war camp in Germany, he too felt the need to stop these rivalries. It's thanks largely to his persistent efforts that it was achieved."

Achieved it certainly was. The Comité's head-quarters, the *Maison du Vin* now stands at the corner of the main square in Bordeaux, not unworthy of its great neighbour, the Opera House of Victor Louis.

Such is the enterprise of Philippe de Rothschild that, not content with fighting his way for forty years into the first category of the clarets,* he for a time acquired an additional interest in champagne, with the old Rheims firm of Ruinart. In 1950 the following advertisement appeared in the French press:

*Since this was written, he has achieved his goal. In June 1973, Mouton was admitted to the First Category, although the old 1855 classification still remains for other wines.

Château Mouton Rothschild
Baron Philippe de Rothschild
propriétaire
PAUILLAC
&
Champagne Ruinart
père et fils
Vicomte G. Ruinart de Brimont
Baron Philippe de Rothschild
associé
RHEIMS
Deux noms prestigieux maintenant unis

A man of many parts, Philippe de Rothschild uses his fortune in other domains than wine-making, particularly in the encouragement of sporting and literary ventures. In his early days, he made his mark in a very different field – motor racing – displaying a skill and daring which impressed even the experts. Today at the age of seventy, much of his energy finds its expression in literature. He translates Elizabethan poetry into French, in what are regarded by the pundits in Paris as definitive versions; and he is the official French translator of the contemporary English dramatist, Christopher Fry, whose complicated bravura style and imagery he has mastered. One of the Baron's own poems was used for the libretto of *Vendanges*, the opera by Darius Milhaud which was performed at Nice.

Next door to Mouton is Château Lafite, perhaps the best known vineyard in the world. It is owned by Philippe de Rothschild's cousins, the Barons Guy and Elie de Rothschild. The former is the Parisian banker and race-horse owner, and he has left the running of the vineyard to Elie. When the Baron Elie took it over after the Second World War, it had suffered not only from the German occupation but from the earlier years of bad vintages and shrinking markets – "the wretched nineteen-thirties" as Mr Cyril Ray calls them in his book *Lafite*, "when poor vintage coincided with the aftermath of the Wall Street crash."

As Mr Ray says further, when the Baron Elie took it over, he was given a stern warning by his banker cousin Guy that even Rothschilds in these times could not go on losing money on a vineyard, and that unless it revived quickly it would have to be sold. Baron Elie now has the satisfaction of recalling that it was in 1948, under his direction, that Lafite paid its first dividend since the Rothschild purchase in 1868.

Mr Frederic Morton in his book *The Rothschilds: a family portrait* describes the Baron Elie as "probably the fiercest, most imperious family members since the first Lord Rothschild". Today aged over fifty, he is still imperious and fierce in his enjoyment of life – a crack shot and a polo player in the international category. Mr Ray relates that when he took over Lafite, he galvanised it, startling and delighting the staff by his ability to both praise and reprimand them in the *argot* of the Médoc.

The Lafite Rothschilds are frequently not in residence (unlike their cousin Philippe at Mouton), and the entertainment and publicity side of the firm is run by M. Guy Schÿler, descendant of the well-known Bordeaux wine family of that name. He told me that the prices obtained today for a bottle of vintage Lafite are astronomic, as much as £50 a bottle – again because of the "wine explosion" since the war, and the huge American demand which outruns the supply.

Like so many of the Bordeaux wine merchants whose families have traded with England for three or four centuries, M. Schÿler is an ardent Anglophile. He possesses every war-time speech of Winston Churchill on gramophone records, and played them to me with greater reverence than would be found in any English home. He is yet another example – to be seen repeatedly in this book – of how the great wine-families, although often in competition commercially, tend to intermarry. His wife is the sister of Madame Pol-Roger, (referred to in the chapter "The Champagne Widows") and she helps him in the entertaining which is the mark of Lafite hospitality. His mother was a Guestier.

He told me how Lafite had, like its neighbour Mouton, been lucky to escape the ravages of war – but this time by good management rather than luck. By June 1940 most of the Rothschilds had either escaped abroad, like Philippe, or were prisoners of war in

Germany (the Baron Elie, a reserve cavalry officer, was captured in the Maginot Line in 1940). In that year the book-keeper at Lafite, Mme Faux, had the foresight to change the labels of those wines belonging to Rothschilds who had joined the Free French – and had therefore, in the eyes of the Vichy government, lost their French nationality – to those of the two brothers, Elie and Alain who, as prisoners of war, were still regarded under the Hague Convention as French. When therefore the Vichy government came to sequestrate the property of all Frenchmen who had emigrated – among them Philippe, Edmond, Maurice and Robert de Rothschild, *"les quatre Juifs déchus de leur nationalité"*, it found that these men owned no wine. The admirable woman also ingeniously transferred over a thousand bottles of the best Lafite from the cellars, where the Germans would look for them, to a remote part of the estate; here they remained undiscovered throughout the war. She stayed at Château Lafite during the war, keeping the books and protecting the interests of the absent Rothschilds. Thanks to her, in 1945 their wines and cellars were intact.

When I said good-bye to Baron Philippe de Rothschild at the gates of Mouton, the *vendange* was in progress. In the fields his workers were slowly moving forward in their serried ranks, waist-deep in the thick foliage of the vines, a marvellous scene of industry, but not – as I said to him – of industry as we know it in the north, marring the face of nature and polluting air and water. No smoking factory here dims the splendour of the sun, no squalor and filth offend the eye.

"You think so, do you?" He caught my arm and, making me half turn towards the east, pointed to some circular metal erections on the distant bank of the Garonne. "That's what this damned French Government has done," he said. "They've allowed an international oil company to set up a refinery here – for a nice sum, you can be sure. But in the Médoc of all places! In time, their excrescences will destroy our precious soil, and that'll be the end of the grape. I've done all I can to get it removed. But I've failed."

Aware that, in the face of international oil interests today, even

Rothschilds are impotent, I sadly took the winding road back to Bordeaux through this wonderful winescape. . . .

At first sight the Médoc, a narrow featureless peninsula running north from Bordeaux for eighty miles to the sea, makes little impression on the newcomer familiar with the other wine lands of France – Burgundy, Provence or Touraine. The eye ranges over mile after mile of gently undulating country, with here and there a wayside shrine, or a dovecote-like tower to announce the marches of some vineyard. The visitor recalling the châteaux of the Loire,

> those castled palaces of France
> shine on the Loire in summer green,

may be disappointed. Every vineyard of note in the Médoc has its château – but not on the scale of Chambord or Chenonceaux. The Médoc soil is too precious to be spared for elaborate building, and most of the wine châteaux are modest country houses. But the names written over their gateways will be as familiar to the wine-lover as those of the great battle-fields of Europe – Lafite, Mouton, Margaux, Latour, Pontet-Canet, Langoa, Pichon-Longueville, Beychevelle. The road winds like a ribbon between the vineyards, and everywhere are the châteaux – some like Beychevelle built in the great period of French architecture, the eighteenth century, others built yesterday by the new rich, with towers and crenellations in imitation of the Middle Ages. One is in the oriental style, and people still ask today to see this "Chinese folly". Château Margaux is also aesthetically bizarre, a vast cube of Empire masonry to which has been bracketed, as if by chance, an Attic pediment supported by hybrid Roman columns and a vast perron as in the Paris Bourse. Every style seems represented – colonnaded façades, majestic flights of steps, mullioned windows. And all around as far as the eye can see an ocean of vines.

7

Cognac —
the Chevalier de la Croix Maron,
Alfred de Vigny, Martel and Courvoisier

Some fifty miles north of Bordeaux, half way between the Garonne and the Loire, lies the department of the Charente, which takes its name from *la molle Charente*, the beautiful and sluggish stream which winds among the meadows and vineyards until it meets the sea at Rochefort. Here is grown a different type of grape, smaller, sourer and used exclusively for producing a distilled, as distinct from fermented, wine – the liquid we call brandy. Its discovery in France dates from much more recent times than that of the fermented grape in Bordeaux.

Here in a village called La Brée in the mid-sixteenth century, the Chevalier Jacques de la Croix Maron retired from active service under Marshal Agrippa d'Aubigny to devote himself to poetry and viticulture. During his campaigning, he had seen that human fatigue could often be combated by liberal potations of the *distilled* juice of the grape. He was familiar with Arnaud de Villeneuve's treatise, *Thresor des Pauvres*, describing how "the most subtle soul of the wine", that is its distilled essence, could cure illness and prolong life – and was therefore known as *eau-de-vie*. Beneficial as the liquid was, its taste was not pleasant, harsh and acrid. The Chevalier planned to spend his retirement producing an *eau-de-vie* from which this flavour would be eliminated, and which would also prolong sexual potency – a subject dear to his heart.

In the undulating and luxuriant countryside of the Charente with its southern facing slopes, he harvested his grapes, set up his alembic and began his experiments in distillation. For several

68

years he had no success; he could not eliminate the acrid flavour, nor did his *eau-de-vie* bestow fresh aphrodisiac powers. At this point fact and fiction became somewhat confused, and the story of the Chevalier's experiments has since been used on several occasions as a theme for fiction (the last being in 1943 when the playwright Eugène Guillebaud depicted Henry of Navarre as a great Cognac drinker).

According to the legend, the Chevalier was visited one stormy night by the Devil, who came to see him in a dream. The Devil said he proposed to boil him alive to see if he could divorce his soul from his body, because he wished to take possession of the former. This unpleasant proposal was put into practice (in the dream) but with only partial success, for the Chevalier's soul still remained tenaciously attached to his body. Whereupon the Devil said, "It is clear that to obtain your soul, I must boil you a second time." This too he was about to do when the Chevalier awoke, shaking and covered with sweat. Fearful as the nightmare was, he immediately realised that he had learned something of great importance for his distillation. The dream had meant that if he was to obtain the "soul" of his wine, he must boil it a second time, that is distil it twice. This he did, thereby inaugurating the process by which brandy has been made ever since, known as *la bonne chauffe*. By distilling it twice, he produced a liquid entirely without the unpalatable flavour of *eau-de-vie*, milder yet of greater alcoholic strength.

Wishing to inform the wine community of his great discovery, he immediately set off for the monks of Renorville, who were great topers, taking with him two casks of Limousin oak containing his new *eau-de-vie*. The monks tasted it, pronounced it the purest nectar that had ever passed their lips, and drank an entire cask. They were about to attack the second cask when the Father Superior, being a provident man, directed that it should be taken from them and hidden in the cellar, lest it should provide too great a temptation. In this way, it lay untouched for fifteen years, until one day the Bishop of Saintes made a pastoral visit. The monks were – unusually for them – without good wine on this important occasion; but one of them remembered the cask with the Chevalier's *eau-de-vie* in the cellar. It was brought up, but on opening it they found, to their dismay, that it was only half full. It was assumed that one of their number had drunk it. After much unavailing recrimination, it was decided that somehow half of the liquid had evaporated. It was then noted that not only had the *eau-de-vie* an indescribably delicious flavour, but that its colour which had been like any *eau-de-vie*, white, was now deep golden. The Bishop tasted it and found the perfume so subtle, the aroma of this "soul of the wine" so delicate, that he went into ecstasies, describing the liquid as "divine". He wanted to proceed immediately to La Brée to bless the discoverer of "the divine fluid"; but this proved impossible, for the good Chevalier had died twelve years before. The Bishop of Saintes could only pronounce a long and eloquent prayer for the soul of this benefactor of the human race.

True or not, the legend describes accurately what had happened – and also how Cognac has been made ever since. The Limousin oak, in which the Chevalier had put it by chance, possesses an aromatic fragrance unknown to any other wood; and it is so coarse-pored that the oxygen in the air has access to the liquid in the cask, which gradually evaporates, removing with it the unpleasant, acrid flavour; while the tannin in the Limousin oak gives it its amber-yellow colour. During those fifteen years, wood and fluid had worked together, as had Chevalier and monk, to produce the finest liqueur in the world.*

So much for the legend. Of the more palpable figures among the Cognac "Princes of the Grape" first place must go to a poet, one of the greatest of the French nineteenth century, Alfred de Vigny. His solicitude for his vineyards and *eau-de-vie* at Maine-Giraud in the Charente can be compared with that of Montesquieu for his claret at La Brède. De Vigny inherited Maine-Giraud from his mother late in life, when he was fifty-five. He was lucky to have inherited it at all, for it was not a family property; his mother had inherited it from her sister who had, in turn, inherited it from her husband, de Baradin, in whose family it had been for centuries.

---

*The oak forests of Limousin lie some fifty miles from Cognac; they were planted by Colbert for a very different purpose, to build men-of-war for the French navy.

Like so many literary men who, when they have become successful in their career, wish to show that socially, too, they are
presentable, de Vigny was most anxious to appear a *grand
seigneur*. In his propertyless days this had been impossible, but
now he was a member of the landed gentry, and he described
his country-house in the documents as a *château-fort*. This was
to overrate both its antiquity and nobility. To regard Maine-Giraud
as even a masterpiece of the Renaissance or the *Grand Siècle* would
require a poet's imagination, not to mention self-deception. It is
no more than a gentleman's small manor house, in a luxuriant
countryside, surrounded by vineyards. However it gave de Vigny
satisfaction, which he appears to have displayed with a certain
arrogance – for the critic Sainte-Beuve describes him as *le poète
hautain* and refers to his *orgeuil de caste*.

In his letters to his agent at Maine-Giraud, the author of *La
Mort du Loup* who, at the late age of fifty-five had become the
proprietor of several fine vineyards and presses, reveals a practical
business sense unusual, indeed almost unbecoming, in a poet. On
12 December 1849, he wrote from Paris, "You have doubtless
begun *la bonne chauffe*. Ensure that during it there is someone
always present, day and night, to extinguish the flame at the
proper moment. . . . I am pleased with the prices we are getting
for the Eau-de-Vie. Call immediately on M. Michaud, the agent
of M. Hennessey at Châteauneuf, and try to sell him our Eau-de-Vie
of this year. Sell the eight barrels if you can at 400 Fr. – more if
you can get it, *but on no account below this price . . .*"

On 20 April 1854, the poet notes, "The price of our Eau-de-Vie
seems pretty reasonable, but it has been a bad year, and M.
Hennessey says there will be neither a rise nor a lowering in
price until the vintage. I shall wait until I hear from you about
the effect of the frosts before fixing a price." This poet-business-
man evidently hoped that the frosts would put the price up – for
he goes on, "I have decided nothing yet with M. Hennessey, but
you are not to deal with anyone else, because I shall probably
decide not to sell this year, and retain all the production, hoping
for a price rise. You will therefore visit the *chais* regularly, to
ensure that evaporation is not too great." On 22 March 1856 he

wrote, "My young friend, M. Ovinde Landry, writes suggesting 230–235 Fr. per hectolitre – but a number of others tell me that the price will probably rise to 250, even perhaps to 260. I have therefore not replied to M. Landry, because you do not tell me *if you think he will go up to this price,* or if M. Hennessey's agents will. Reply by return with the difference in prices quoted per hectolitre – of both my oldest Eau-de-Vie and the new one..." On 21 February 1857 he launches into technical details: "I prefer you to buy wood rather than peat for the burning, although the latter is cheaper – but I think it effects the taste.... Sell a few barrels, then find out the *probability of a rise* in price. If it is regarded as certain, stop the sale and wait for the rise.... You tell me that one of my neighbours, M. Blair, is selling at 200 Fr. per barrel to 'well-known firms'. That is too low. But you must give me more precise details. It is not enough to talk of 'well-known' firms. I want their names, above all the credit they possess ..."

In these later years of his life, de Vigny appears to have been a good landlord, conscious of his new responsibilities as a country gentleman, anxious to learn every detail about wine making, and the mentality and problems of his *vignerons.* In his letters to his agent, he is constantly referring to the education of their children and the state of their health. In short, he lived up to the image he had formed of himself, and he paid eloquent tribute to the land of his adoption in the famous lines:

> *Il est une contrée où France est bacchante,...*
> *Où la liqueur de feu mûrit au grand soleil,...*
> *Où des volcans éteints frémit la cendre ardente,...*
> *Où l'esprit des vins aux laves est pareil....**

In the late seventeenth century the new class of *négociants* was also settling in the Cognac region, most of them, as in Bordeaux, of Anglo-Irish origin. The two biggest today, Hennessey and Martell came from, respectively, Ireland and the Channel Islands. The Martells attached such importance to their British origins

---

*Literal translation: In the province of France which is Bacchus's votary, a fiery liquid matures in the fullness of the sun, where dead volcanoes make the burning cinders quiver, where the spirit of subtle wine belongs to the lava.

that they added an "l" to the original "Martel", because the double "l" is clearly a British termination.

Today Martell, together with Hennessey and Courvoisier, share eighty per cent of the total production of cognac. Like Moët et Chandon in Champagne, they have a guest house château just outside Cognac, where their hospitality is legendary. On its English lawns strut peacocks, and on the lake are swans. The firm has its private aeroplane in which the Directors fly to Paris and other commercial centres; the train, they say, is too slow. Since the Second World War, the Brandy trade has become highly competitive; so the American "Time is Money" axiom has reappeared beside the sleepy waters of the Charente.

M. Michel Martell, one of the directors, told me that the consumption of cognac has risen considerably in the ten years between 1960 and 1970, from 10 million bottles to 24 million. This is largely due to the expanding American market. Once again, as in Bordeaux, America is influencing the wine trade of Europe increasingly every year. The American whisky firms of Hiram Walker and Seager have bought up, respectively, Courvoisier and Augier, while the English Distilling Company Ltd have bought up the old Cognac firm of Hine. Martini has taken over Gaston Legrange, and Hennessey has joined with Möet et Chandon. M. Martell was proud to say that of the big houses only his remains independent, as it has since 1715.

He took me round the *chais* and told me that the most important man in a cognac firm is the *maître de chais* because, as all cognacs are blended (which is not necessarily the case with wines), he alone is responsible for the quality. These men are born to the craft, and most of them come from a long line of tasters. The *maître* at Martell, M. François Chapeau, represents the sixth generation of tasters of his family in the direct male line. At Hennessey, M. Fillious is also of the sixth generation, while at Augier the *maître* is of the seventh. Like their ancestors, these men spend their entire lives, from boyhood, sipping and sniffing at little glasses; so delicate is their palate that not only can they judge exactly what blends best, but they can discern to within a degree if the temperature of the *bonne chauffe* has been too high or too low, if the grape has been picked before or after it is ripe, even if there is something wrong in the shape of the still. The most eloquent features of their rubicund physiognomy are the nostrils and lips, thin, twitching and slightly disdainful.

When John Martell from the Channel Islands founded his firm in 1715 there was little competition. He settled at first in Bordeaux as a *négociant en vins*, like the Barton and Johnstons. Unlike these Anglo-Irish however, his wine affairs did not prosper, and he soon removed to Cognac, where he set up in the newly developing Eau-de-Vie business. An impediment to his initial success was his Protestant faith which he obstinately refused to renounce, marrying one of the Protestants in Cognac, the daughter of a prosperous Doctor. The Martell family history reveals that all their childrens' baptismal documents were drawn up by a Catholic *curé* who noted that the parents could not appear at the ceremony on account of their faith. They had to absent themselves to avoid the regulations which then denied them all *état civil*, and to prevent their children having the title "bastard", with disastrous consequences for their civil position. Nevertheless, such was this first Martell's industry that by his death thirty years later, he had one of the most flourishing firms in Cognac.

The most picturesque member of the Martell family was John Martell's ninth child, Théodore. His fame, like that of Hugh Barton, is connected with French Revolution, for, as we have seen, the Revolutionaries regarded the prosperous wine-merchants as *ci-devants*. He was arrested in 1793, when Tallien arrived in Gascony as pro-Consul, and the heads began to fall. He was put on trial for what were, in terms of Revolutionary ethics, grave charges – speculation on the Bordeaux stock-exchange and intelligence with London. Most sinister of all, he was accused that in a business letter he had referred to "the sad event of the 21 January". (the execution of Louis XVI). His speculations in wine on the stock exchange had, it was alleged, caused the "price of the commodity to rise", and he had used secret information from the bankers in London, to make large killings on the stock exchange. The Revolutionaries had seized quantities of letters and documents from his office, on which they based their charges.

Martell defended himself stoutly. To the most serious charge, that he had referred in a letter to "the sad event of the 21st January", he explained that it had been written by one of his clerks, Herzog, a foreigner with insufficient knowledge of the French language, and that all he had meant was that it was a sad thing that a French King should have brought himself to such a sorry pass. The revolutionary Tribunal sat for two days, and then stated, "We have carefully studied the correspondence of the accused wine-merchant, Théodore Martell, from whose letters it is proved beyond doubt that English bankers were in the habit of sending him information by special messengers about operations on the stock exchange. One letter leaves no doubt as to his attitude towards the death of the last tyrant of the French. We are prepared to accept, however, his explanation that it was written by the clerk, Herzog, whose knowledge of French was limited. In his commercial dealings in the wine-trade, however, he is guilty of most venal ambition and gross selfishness – qualities displayed, alas, all too often in businessmen!" The Tribunal sentenced him to a fine of 150,000 livres.

Although a large sum, this seems, for 1793 with the Terror at its height, a surprisingly lenient sentence, and lends credence to the theory that the Comtesse de Fontenay had used her influence with her lover, Tallien, to save Martell from the guillotine. This is confirmed in the famous Memoirs of the Marquise de la Tour du Pin, who writes that one evening she found the Comtesse de Fontenay alone, "in great trouble and anxiety. She was walking up and down the room, and the least noise set her trembling. She explained that M. Martell, a brandy dealer, to whose wife and children she was most attached, was at that moment before the Tribunal. She said that although Tallien had promised her that he would save him, she feared that his fanatical colleague, Ysabeau, would have Martell executed. Eventually, after an hour of almost convulsive impatience, we heard someone running in our direction. She became terribly pale. The door opened and a breathless man gasped, 'He's escaped the guillotine. Only a fine.' It was Tallien's secretary." (Later, Mme de Fontenay married Tallien.)

In the nineteenth and twentieth centuries, the affairs of the

Martell firm prospered greatly, principally due to the Trade Treaty negotiated by Napoleon III with England, by which French brandy received preferential treatment. During this hundred years, the Martell archives yield little of interest, save continual references to increased profits and growing trade with countries as distant as China and Japan. Even the First World War seems to have affected Martell hardly at all – they were so remote from the front (unlike the Champagne firms, which were ruined). Things were very different however in the Second World War, when the whole of Gascony was occupied by the Germans. They bought large consignments of brandy for their Armed Forces at the unfavourable rate of exchange they had imposed on the conquered country. Fortunately for Martell, the German officer in charge of these transactions with the brandy firms was von Klebich who had, before 1939, been the Martell representative in Hamburg. He naturally wished to favour his old firm, and offered tempting terms to Martell to supply virtually the entire Germany army with brandy. The Martell chairman, who was also Mayor of Cognac, was wise enough to refuse this attractive offer, insisting that the tenders must be put out to *all Cognac firms*. He was far-sighted enough to believe, even in 1940, that Germany would not win the war, and that the Liberation would not be indulgent to any firms who had profited from the Occupation.

Another old *négociant* family – again of Anglo-Irish origin – is that of Otard. The name, in spite of its *roturier* flavour, is Scots in origin and probably the most aristocratic in the whole of Gascony. Its founder accompanied William the Conqueror to England, where he and his descendants acquired a host of feudal titles, including that of Baron of Dum-Ottard and the Grange in Scotland, and Seigneur de la Motte-Saint Privat in Périgord, and of Mérignac in France.At one stage, they became Irish Barons O'Tard. Their Cognac firm was founded much later, in 1795 in association with Jean Dupuy, the son of a local notary, as Otard, *Dupuy et Cie*. They acquired the Château de Cognac, the birthplace of François I. Four generations of Otards directed the firm until 1967, when the male line became extinct. The widow (who was the mother of Boni de Castellane) ran the firm for two years, and then sold it to the family of Durand de Ramefort and the Société St Raphaël, who are the present distributors of Otard brandy.

The Cognac family probably best known to the English speaking world is that of Hennessey. In 1740, Richard Hennessey, third son of Charles Hennessey, squire of Ballymacmoy in County Cork, while fighting in the Clare Regiment for the King of France, was wounded near Cognac. He settled there, took a liking to the local Eau-de-Vie, and sent a few casks to friends and relations at home. They approved of it so enthusiastically that he founded a small firm for exporting it, in 1765. Today it is, with Martell, the biggest brandy firm in France. Six generations of Hennesseys have followed the founder whose son Jacques (significantly, he had already taken a French Christian name and nationality), was elected to the House of Representatives under the Revolution. However, they quickly adapted themselves to the Restoration, and flourished during the nineteenth century. Today the Hennesseys are almost as famous for their racing stud as for their brandy. They owned the only French horse ever to win the Grand National, and they were the first firm to sponsor a steeplechase in England, the Hennessey Gold Cup.

The third big brandy firm today is Courvoisier. It is of Swiss origin, although there appears to be some difficulty in tracing the line to the founder of the firm. There is a tradition that Napoleon I used to drink only Courvoisier brandy on his campaigns. It appears certain that he drank some form of Cognac, and even had casks of cognac on the *Bellerephon* when he went into exile; Cognac was also certainly on his menus in the Tuileries, Saint-Cloud and Malmaison. Courvoisier brandy is known to have been supplied to his Marshal, Soult, but the rest is largely conjecture. What is certain is that Napoleon appointed Félix Courvoisier of Jarnac *"seul fournisseur"* of brandy to the Imperial Court and made him commander of the National Guard in Paris. To that extent then, Courvoisier may be described as "the brandy of Napoleon" a publicity device with which the firm makes great play today.

Courvoisier himself appears to have disappeared about 1890

without heirs, and in 1910 the firm was bought by Simon Brothers. Like Martell, they flourished until the Second World War, when the Germans occupied their château in Jarnac, and turned it into an Officers' Club. The Germans contended that because the proprietor's name was now Simon, they must be Jewish, and that the firm of Courvoisier was, according to their anti-Semitic laws, to be sequestrated. The present Chairman, M. Braastad, ingeniously managed to convince them, with the help of entries in the Simon family Bible, that the Simons were of unimpeachable Aryan origin, and the sequestration order was rescinded. In 1964 the firm was sold again, this time to Hiram Walker, the American whisky magnate, in whose possession it remains today.

8

The English in Oporto —
Baron Forrester

Armed with letters of introduction, I now proceeded southward from Bordeaux over the Pyrenees to Oporto, where the vintage takes place later in the year, and where a very different type of "Prince of the Grape" was to be my host. He is best described by Hector Bolitho who, of the long railway journey up into the Alto Douro where the port vines grow, wrote:

> "I found myself travelling through a completely wild and exotic landscape in a compartment with two Old Etonian wine-merchants, a young man with an Old Wellingtonian tie, and an English lady dressed as if for the Cheltenham Gold Cup. After a few stops two more passengers got in; they were both Oporto wine-merchants one of whom, I learnt, had been at school at Rugby, and the other had played rugger for Wales. When I reached my destination, the Quinta where I was to view the vintage, I smelled outside my bedroom window the eucalyptus and orange trees; but otherwise, the house in which I stayed might have been an English country-house, with copies of *The Times* and the *Illustrated London News* on the tables, and Surtees hunting prints on the walls. . . ."

I was to have the opportunity in Oporto of confirming for myself this marked "Englishness" of the port wine firms, which seem all to be called Taylor, Cobb or Robertson. The city possesses such English institutions as its own cricket club, golf club, tennis club, rowing club, a preparatory school run on the lines of The Dragon, Oxford, and the British Seamens' Rest – the last founded by the wine merchants in collaboration with the YMCA. The prep

79

school prepares the youth of the English colony for the English public schools, where their fathers and grandfathers, all port wine merchants, were educated before them. As Marie Noele Kelly writes in her informative book about Portugal. "Port became in the 18th century as it were a sort of honorary British citizen. . . . The red-faced and pink-coated English squires would lay down the port to mature against the heir's coming of age . . ."*

We cannot explain this English domination of the port wine trade by simply saying that port was originally an Englishman's drink, and that naturally Englishmen would come out here to make it.† For it is also a lucrative drink. Why therefore did the Portuguese not make more of their own soil, for they were enterprising and adventurous enough when it came to colonies overseas? Some say that only the phlegmatic English would take the trouble to make the difficult eighty mile journey into the inhospitable Alto Douro, whose vineyards alone yield the heavy mahogany liquid called port. It appears, too, that the Portuguese, good sailors as they were, were apprehensive about the unmanageable river Douro with its gorges blocked by rocks and rapids, which have claimed thousands of victims.

Richard Ford, writing a hundred and fifty years ago on his travels, attributes it all to Iberian sloth. He says that because Nature is so lavish in these parts, no Portuguese or Spaniard can be bothered to get anything which Nature does not bring to him. "He will drink wine," Ford writes, "if it is on his doorstep. If it isn't, he will make do with water. The most celebrated wines of the Peninsula," he continues, "are Port and Sherry, which owe their excellence to foreign, not native skill." Certainly, the early English port wine merchants must have been a tough lot. The journey up the Douro to the wine Quintas then took three days and the inns were little better than shacks. Often they had to spend the night – in the words of a seventeenth-century contemporary – "sleeping on ye tables for reason of ye insects".

Not all the English families who settled here, mostly in the

*This Delicious Land – Portugal. Hutchinson, 1956.
†For another excellent description of Oporto and the port wine trade, see Sarah Bradford's The Englishman's Wine.

eighteenth century, who founded firms with the famous names, Taylor, Fladgate, Phayre, Croft, Warre, have survived down to our own times. The best known among them today, although not the oldest, is Sandeman, which is run in Oporto by Mr Glyn Jennings, also a descendant of a distinguished port family. His gentle, quiet-voiced manner – typical of the English public-school vintner – conceals a powerful personality and the self-confidence of a man who knows the business as well as anyone in Portugal. He told me that since the Second World War the emphasis has changed completely. "As you know," he said, "port has for centuries been made for the English market – moreover the *quality* English market. The vintage port you get in the London clubs. But this market has now shrunk, and today eighty percent of our production goes to France, where it is drunk as an aperitif called Porto."

Although he obviously would not admit it, he must be distressed by this, because French Porto is an insipid liquid, a pale imitation of the real thing. I asked him how he accounted for this, and he said that: first, the market for it among the French *petite bourgeoisie* has increased greatly since the war; it is considered good form among them to drink a glass of Porto before a meal. "Secondly, alas," he said, "the English gentleman, the squire and the fox-hunting parson, have declined. There is no one now in the Pall Mall clubs to boast, like Dr Johnson, that he can drink three bottles of vintage port at a sitting." The old Meredith adage about port, "Sound and Senatorial", no longer holds.

Nevertheless, his firm has adapted itself to changed circumstances. In such a conservative and traditional trade as that of port wine, his firm was considered immensely daring to introduce modern methods of advertisement. They invented, for example, the company's now famous "Don" trade mark. "At the time," I was told, "certain members of the trade considered this immensely vulgar. A good wine needs no bush, they said. But the fact is, it tripled our sales."

Mr Glyn Jennings is typical of the Oporto "Princes of the Grape". Not for them the palaces and châteaux of the Médoc and Champagne, the stud farms and race-horses, but comfortable

dwellings in the residential quarter of Oporto with perhaps a summer house in the Minho up the coast, with sailing, swimming and
golf for relaxation. In summer, too, you will see the English wine-
merchants in their off hours sitting in the shade near the Carrana
palace watching their cricket team playing the visiting Harlequins
or the MCC under Colonel Leveson-Gower; while the local
Portuguese look on in amazement at this curious game, fearing
that at any moment it may lead to bloodshed. Legend relates that
on one occasion the Queen of Portugal accepted an invitation to
watch the English wine-merchants playing cricket (for the
Portuguese Royal Family were always prepared to patronise
British "cultural activities", as cricket was for some reason termed).
She arrived when one side had just been bowled out, and their
opponents had started to bat. She became so fascinated by the
incomprehensible antics of the players that she asked if, as she
had missed the "first act", the cast would be willing to play it
again for her.

Also befitting the English public-school tradition, the English
wine-merchants have their own exclusive club, "The Factory
House", for which unsuitable candidates are blackballed. The
term "Factory" in its conventional sense hardly does justice to the
grandeur and elegance of this eighteenth-century building. The
word "Factory" is assumed by most people today to be connected
with manufacturing. But in the British trading stations scattered
all over the world in the colonial days, the word derived from
"Factor", an agent acting on behalf of firms at home. The Oxford
Dictionary defines it as "a merchant company's foreign trading
station".

The Factory House was built in 1790. It is on three floors with
a mezzanine between the ground floor and the *piano nobile*. The
ground floor is in the form of a Palladian rusticated loggia, divided
into seven openings, their dispositions being repeated in the upper
stories. With its broad perspective of solid granite and rows of
iron-balconied windows and cornices, it is a symbol of all that
is solid and respectable in British commerce.

Those wine merchants who are "Partners" – that is, heads of the
great firms like Sandeman, Croft, Taylor, Dow and so on – are *ex-*

1 The statue of Dom
Pérignon at his birth-
place near Rheims

2 Philippe, Régent
d'Orléans

3 La Duchesse de Berry

4 A *Petit Souper* at the
Palais Royal – early
eighteenth century

5 La Veuve Clicquot

6 Jean-Remy Moët welcoming Napoleon I in his cellars at Épernay

NAPOLÉON IER VISITANT LES CAVES DE MOËT & CHANDON, LE 26 JUILLET 1807

7 Isabey's Orangery at
Moët et Chandon,
Épernay

8 The Marne countryside

9 A Revolutionary caricature, 'Le nouveau pressoir du clergé'

10 Montesquieu, Baron de la Brède

11 Richard Hennessey – founder of the brandy firm

12 Victor Louis's *Grand Théâtre* in Bordeaux

13 Chancellor Rollin of Burgundy

14 The port of Bordeaux in the eighteenth century

15 Baron Philippe de Rothschild in his vineyards at Mouton

16 A sixteenth century tapestry from the wine museum, Mouton

17 Château Lafite

18 Grapes coming into the *chais* at Château Yquem

19 Alfred de Vigny

21 The wine-
merchants'
Factory House in
Oporto

22 Baron Bettino
Ricasoli

20 *opposite* The river
Douro with its
terraced vineyards

23 Schloss Vollrads

24 Schloss Johannisberg

26 *opposite above* Uprooting the vines in Gaul, at the orders of the
Emperor Domitian AD 92
27 *opposite below* Ausonius, the Latin poet of Bordigala (Bordeaux)

25 *below* Tombs of the Burgundian Dukes in the *Salle des Gardes*, Dijon

28 Horace's Sabine farm

29 The banks of the Garonne

officio members of the Factory House. For generations they have crossed its arcaded and iron-trellised threshold and traversed its vaulted vestibule to mount the great granite staircase. Here I was escorted into the dessert-room on the first floor between the banqueting-hall and the great Ionic pillared ballroom. In this Holy of Holies of the port wine hierarchy, standing at the long mahogany table extending the length of the room, I saw these men, whose noses and palates have been trained by decades of sniffing and sipping, nodding sagely to one another over crystal goblets containing the new vintage.

No Portuguese can become a member of the Factory House, although they are occasionally invited there. At a party to which I was invited, I saw a small swarthy man in a corner of the room looking rather sorry for himself. I asked a member of the Factory House who he was, and was told, "He's feeling a bit out of it because he's the only Portuguese here."

When I was in Oporto, I heard of no blackballing from the Factory House of unsuitable English candidates but I learnt that in their time the now highly respected port wine firms of Cockburn and Graham had suffered that fate. It was after the Peninsular War, when a host of new names appeared on the shippers' list. The older members regarded the newcomers as "Johnny-come-latelys", who required a generation or two before they were fit to enter the Holy of Holies of portocracy. One of their principal objections to the newcomers was that these men, like Graham, traded not only in wine – a gentlemanly occupation – but also in hardware, nuts, bolts, textiles and so forth. The new men, for their part, considered that by their enterprise in building new firms they had contributed more to the commerce between England and Portugal than had their seniors. They contended that the Factory House, towards whose upkeep all British merchants in Oporto paid their dues, was a national institution which should be open to all British merchants trading in Oporto. The dispute reached such proportions that the newcomers applied to the Foreign Secretary himself. "The Factory House members," they wrote, "seek to monopolise the advantages they enjoy by means of certain regulations which prevent any application for admission on our part, by the obnoxious mode of decision by ballot whereby a black ball affords to the secret hand of individual resentment or caprice the power to stigmatise any applicant by partial and unjust seclusion."

In spite of all these representations, the new men obtained no satisfaction from the Foreign Office. To this day, the Factory House remains the preserve of members of the wine trade, and merchants in other commodities are not admitted – although of course wine-shippers like Cockburn and Graham have long become highly respected members.

It is much the same today as yesterday, when Costigin could write in 1842 in his *Sketches of Society and Manners in Portugal*, "The English wine merchants in Oporto are a worthy, friendly and hospitable set of gentlemen; many of them have been 20 or 30 years in the country and know only a few words of the language . . ." In general, the English wine merchants still do not intermarry with the Portuguese, nor do they make much attempt at establishing friendship with the Portuguese upper classes. Indeed, the life of that class in the past must have seemed very odd to them.

The Fidalgos – as the Portuguese aristocracy are called – lived in their tumbledown palaces surrounded by hordes of priests, grooms, dwarfs, mistresses, dogs, legitimate children, illegitimate children, elderly relations and innumerable servants, the latter treated as familiars. Tea, gambling, dancing and making love occupied most of their day; to them the very idea of making money through trade – *selling* wine – seemed preposterous. It is understandable, therefore, that the English have taken almost complete charge of the wine business in northern Portugal.

There is however one important exception to this curious state of affairs: the Portuguese firm of Ferreira. I was entertained by them in their lavish board-room on the riva di Gaia, where they proudly discoursed on their famous ancestor, the great lady who founded their firm. "Yes, it was a woman," I was told, to my amazement. "And today we still have women in the firm – not as mere employees, but as Directors. They have a head for figures."

The remarkable lady in question is Doña Antonia Ferreira, whose long sallow face and bright black eyes look down disdainfully from the big portrait hanging today in the board-room. A mystery surrounds her birth. "All we know," I was told, "is that she had the happy knack of marrying rich men. Under her influence, they lavished most of their wealth on acquiring and developing vineyards in the Alto Douro." My informant, one of the younger directors, spoke excellent English, as befitting a man who visits our island twice a year for contracts. "Her first husband, Bernado Ferreira," he explained, "was what you would call today a 'playboy'. He built a magnificent palace on the largo de Trinidade, the smartest square in Oporto, which occupied an entire side of that square – with ballrooms, dining-rooms, supper-rooms in blue, white, green and yellow. But thanks to Doña Antonia Ferreira, was not squandered on entertainments and the gaming tables – but on developing and expanding their vineyards in the Douro."

When he died, she inherited these vineyards and then immediately married another rich man, Senhor Torres, whom she persuaded in much the same way to spend his money on buying the great Vesuvio vineyards, still today the largest and finest in the Douro. When he died, Doña Antonia inherited these and spent the rest of her life there, ruling her twelve quintas as a benevolent dictator. Her thousands of acres were her only thought, and her choice of stewards proved what an excellent busineswoman she was. She possessed such a vast estate that her daughter was able to marry the Count of Azambuja, son of the Infanta of Portugal.

The English domination of the Oporto wine business is at last being challenged by other Portuguese firms. It is fitting to close this account of the Oporto shippers with a modern Portuguese firm, which has the greatest record of success in the entire European wine industry since the Second World War – Mateus. This rosé wine in the familiar flagon bottle with the Mateus Palace label has, almost literally, swamped the rosé markets of the world within the last fifteen years, since its invention in 1947. Forty-four million bottles of this pink and sparkling fluid are drunk annually all over the world, from Oporto to San Francisco and Tokyo. It is all due to the genius of one man, Fernando van-Zeller Guedes, whom I had the privilege of meeting during my last week in Oporto.

The Guedes are an old Portuguese family which has long owned vineyards in the Alto Douro, but which had by the end of the First World War declined to a state verging almost on bankruptcy. The young son, Fernando – the man I have referred to – was accordingly packed off to London to work in a subordinate position in a wine firm to learn the business. Although, as he said, he learnt a great deal, he does not appear to have prospered in England; by the end of the Second World War, after twenty years in the firm, when he asked for a modest rise in salary it was refused.

He is a tall distinguished-looking man, who told me, "I returned disconsolate to Oporto." Nevertheless this was his opportunity for, working on his own under no master, he discovered where his true talents lay. He suddenly realised that in the post-1945 world advertisement and publicity were the secret of commercial success. He hit upon the brilliant idea of bottling some of the rosé wine from the broken down family estates in an unusually shaped flagon, and putting a label on it which would appeal to the more romantically minded customers. The most beautiful Baroque building in northern Portugal, the Mateus Palace, is on the threshold of the Alto Douro. Its present owners appear to have some distant relationship with the Guedes, so Fernando Guedes placed a coloured picture of its façade on his bottle. The wine found favour with the Portuguese who have in any case always preferred light wines. But it was not until 1951 when the English writer, Sacheverell Sitwell, praised it in a Sunday newspaper that it began to sell in Britain.

"Whatever Britain did or did not do for me in my apprenticeship," said Senior Guedes, "I regard it as the wine shop-window of the world. And so it proved."

Clever publicity did the rest, and although it is in no way an outstanding wine its Baroque label is today probably the best known bottle in the world. The annual sale of 44 million bottles surpasses that of all the other wine shippers of Oporto put together, multiplied several times over. Sacheverell Sitwell clearly should be made an honorary director of the firm and given one year's production free.

I said goodbye to the peculiar tumble-down charm of Oporto

with some regret. With its many churches and public buildings towering above one another in irregular tiers along a precipitous cliff above the Douro, it is a jumble of old houses with belvederes, pointed, projecting roofs, gaily coloured façades and lines of ornamental balconies, with washing hanging from them in profusion. The port wine trade is centred principally in its suburb, Vila Nova da Gaia on the left bank of the river, in huge "Lodges", in each of which some 150,000 pipes of wine are stored. Here on my last day I was entertained in the Sandeman lodge. It is one of the finest pieces of eighteenth-century architecture in Oporto, and the Sandemans are the only old established firm which has never moved from these, their original premises. It is symbolic of Oporto that this example of the Palladian style should have been imported here like so much else that is English by the great John Carr of York.

Historically the most outstanding figure in the Oporto wine trade was also an Englishman, John James Forrester, who spent most of his life in the country, finishing up with a fortune and a Portuguese barony. The name of this man, who was born in Hull in 1815, is so intimately connected with Portuguese viticulture that he is claimed as much by the Portuguese as by his own countrymen. No one, since port wine was first shipped, has worked harder for it, both scientifically and commercially. A man of many parts, at once wine-merchant,* oenologist, cartographer, landscape painter and writer, his greatest achievement on behalf of the Oporto wine trade was his map of the river Douro, and the vineyards on its steep slopes. Although then completely uncharted, it was the only highway by which the wine could reach Oporto, eighty miles away, brought down in the curiously shaped caique boats. This was a considerable feat, for the Douro was then far less navigable than it is today, and its sinister gorge, the Cachao de Valleira, was choked with rocks. Even today after their removal, the trip can be made only with an experienced boatman, for it abounds in rapids. In the spring when the snows melt, the river becomes a raging torrent of foaming waves, sweeping away

*He worked in his uncle's port shipping firm, Ottley and Forrester (now part of Sandeman).

everything in its path, boats, cattle, men.

Forrester wrote a number of learned treatises on viticulture, among them, in the 1850s when the *Odium Tuckerei* scourge was destroying the Douro vineyards, his *Illustrated Paper on the Wine Diseases of the Alto Douro*. In this he described the disease so precisely that it could be controlled, and later eliminated. His other works on the wine trade include a study of diseases in vine leaves, an essay, *The Effect of high Duties on the wines of Portugal*, and *Essay showing the prejudicial effect of monopoly on the Portuguese wine trade*. In the field of painting, his landscapes of the Douro, depicting its vineyards as well as its wild and majestic scenery, have not been surpassed by any native painter. For these achievements he was elected a member of the Royal Academies of Lisbon and Oporto; and in 1855, the King of Portugal created him a baron of the realm.

By a fearful irony this man who had, as it were, tamed the dreaded Douro with his map, finished his life as another of its victims. In the summer of 1861, after visiting his vineyards in the Douro to pay his workmen, he was descending the river in a caique, in the company of three ladies, one of whom was the famous Dona Antonia Ferreira. Rumour had it that he was comforting her in her second widowhood. On approaching the rapids, the boatman did not lash the rudder. When Baron Forrester with his practised eye noticed this, he remarked to one of the ladies that he feared something might go wrong. He did not speak in time, for at that moment the boat swung athwart the current and capsized. The ladies of the party were miraculously saved by the voluminous crinolines and petticoats they were wearing, on which they floated to shore. But Forrester, whose belt was crammed with the gold coins for paying his workmen, sank and was drowned. When his body was recovered, it was found that the coins which had weighed him down, and which had caused his death, had been stolen from his corpse. His death is still considered something of a mystery in Opórto.

9

The Spanish Sherry Barons
Domecq and Gonzalez

If in Oporto the wine potentates frankly admit their English trading origins, in Spain, where the principal wine families are Spanish, everyone claims to be noble. All the great sherry firms of Jerez describe themselves in their sales brochures as "Ancient and Noble". The name of one of the greatest, Gonzalez, for instance, represents all that is noblest in Spain. Count Fernan Gonzalez was the founder of the Castilian dynasty, and every Spaniard bearing that name claims descent from the hero of Cascajares (in much the same way that all Campbells consider themselves cousins of the Duke of Argyll). True or not, it is a splendid tradition, and every sherry firm today has a magnificent and richly quartered coat of arms prominently displayed on every item connected with sales.

Add to these lofty aspirations the Spanish flair for display, and it is not hard to understand how Julian Pemartin, who in a decade made a million out of sherry, took to living literally as a "Prince of the Grape". In Jerez he built himself not a house but a palace, on the lines of Garnier's Opera House in Paris, where he entertained on a lavish scale. Among his guests was the King of Spain. At a magnificent ball given for the monarch, this sherry potentate asked if anything in the entertainment was lacking. The King replied that it was truly regal, that nothing appertaining to the royal status had been neglected. Whereupon Pemartin said, "Your Majesty is mistaken. One thing is lacking – a rope to hang myself with. I am a ruined man." And so it proved. Shortly afterwards he went bankrupt, and the English firm of Sandeman bought him up, or what remained of him – his *bodegas*, *soleras* and vineyards. His great palace stands today in delapidated splendour on the outskirts of Jerez, inhabited by a colony of peasants whose washing hangs from the ornate balconies.

Greatest today of the Spanish sherry families are the Domecqs, who proudly claim that in the reign of Ferdinand VII the King conferred on them the right of uniting the Royal arms with the firm's trademark. In their sales brochure they refer to "Our ancestor, the noble Juan de Domecq, Seigneur d'Usquain in the district of Béarn, whose device illustrates the symbols of nobility and valour. The word Domecq," the brochure continues, "comes from the language of Oc, translated from the Latin *dominus* which in the Middle Ages established the rights of seigniory. The white gloves of the open hand in the coat of arms set on either side of the drawn sword signify nobility and justice." The head of the firm today is Don Pedro Domecq y Rivero, Marquis of Casa Domecq and Marquis de Domecq d'Usquain, owner of the great mansion in the centre of Jerez, a palace fit for a king with its marble patio and arcaded courts of Moorish paving and sculptured fountains. Elaborate escutcheons figure above the ornamental doorways and the stone pillars have richly carved capitals.

Today the Domecq family in its many ramifications, with innumerable nephews and nieces all intermarried into the big landed estates, forms a little kingdom of its own; and the statue of its greatest member, Pedro Domecq, in one of the main squares dominates the town as much as does that of Primo de Rivera, the Spanish Dictator of the Twenties, who was also a native of Jerez. The managing Director of Domecq today is the youthful and good-looking Don José-Ignazio Domecq whose tremendous energy is divided between the office stool and the polo field. His English is so impeccable and, in equestrian matters, so idiomatic that, were it not for the Spanish polish of his manners, one could easily mistake him for a British "Backwoodsman" peer, one of those convivial characters whose life is divided between the grouse moor and the hunting field. He is today the uncrowned king of the Spanish polo field with a handicap of seven, which puts him in the top international class, among those polo paladins, the Argentinians.

Characteristic of sherry magnates like José-Ignazio Domecq is that, although they indulge wholeheartedly their love of expensive sports (in summer he sails his yacht from the Gulf of Cadiz through the Straits of Gibraltar), they are also dedicated to their work. Jose-Iganzio Domecq is always at his office desk by 8.30 am and, although he comes back to his palacio for lunch, he is back again in the office until dusk.

He told me that their main problem today is to keep prices down because, since the Second World War, great social changes have taken place in Spain. "Although we haven't yet got a welfare state," he said, "I'm glad to say that the condition of the Spanish vineyard workers has improved out of all recognition. All the big sherry firms have introduced a form of social insurance for their workers, sports and amenities and so on. This of course costs more and makes our produce sometimes uncompetitive with that of other countries like South Africa which produce what they have the impertinence to call sherry." It was for this reason, he said, that his firm recently brought a law suit against these countries – with the result that they were henceforth obliged by law to preface the name "Sherry" on their bottles with the adjective of origin – *South African* Sherry, *Australian* Sherry, *Cypriot* Sherry.

I was taken round his great *bodega* on the outskirts of Jerez by one of his nephews who expatiated as we went round on the modern methods introduced by his uncle since 1945. "Sherry has been made in Jerez, since Phoenician times," he explained. "And the methods didn't really change much until recently. For instance, the solera blending process is about the only old method we still retain – by which new wine is continually blended with old wine in these great oak butts. It is centuries old." He stopped and tapped one of the butts in which this process still goes on; and then pointed to something quite different in appearance – "That's a pneumatic grape press. Rather different from the old way of pressing with the bare feet, isn't it? And yet foot pressing went on until well into the twenties. All our bottling is automatic now. And we spray the vineyards from helicopters."

Modern methods may well have been introduced in recent years, but this great Domecq *bodega* still possesses an almost religious

91

atmosphere, as if we were standing in some ancient cathedral. Its five huge naves are separated by four rows of columns between which lie the casks, on their sides, in tiers, thousands of them, a silent congregation, all swollen with the ardent blood of their stomachs, a veritable tidal-wave of alcohol, enough to deprive the entire population of the town of its senses.

Some of them – which he indicated to me – were labelled with illustrious names and coats-of-arms. On one was the name "Napoleon", and he explained that the habit of writing names on certain butts was inaugurated by Marshal Soult in 1808. "After tasting the oldest wines the Marshal, by way of compliment, scrawled the name of his master ... you see, there, Napoleon! We have preserved it under glass."

On other butts I saw scrawled very different names, those of the great Corsican's enemies: Pitt, Nelson, Wellington, even "Georgius Quartus Rex", the first gentleman of Europe, head of the anti-Napoleonic coalition. I asked how they had got there. The reason was simple enough. "Well, business is business," he said. "When Napoleon lost we adapted ourselves to the new condition. After all, England has always been our biggest market."

The reason for this "Vicar of Bray" conduct became apparent to me a few days later when I was given a booklet describing the history of the Domecq family. Although now blessed with a galaxy of titles, the firm started in a humble enough way. It was founded in 1740 by an Irish farmer named Murphy, trading not in wine, but as a general merchant in linen and drapery – and the Domecq connection came later through the distaff side. Murphy became associated with a Frenchman called Haurie who had a small vineyard near Jerez. When Murphy died, Haurie inherited a flourishing business, and he decided to invest all the capital in his vineyard and expand it. Now comes the Domecq connection. Haurie had four nephews who helped him with the viticulture, one of whom had married a daughter of the Domecqs, a family of French origin from the Basses-Pyrénées who had emigrated to Spain in the eighteenth century. These Haurie nephews ran the business until the Peninsular War, when the senior Haurie got into serious trouble for siding with the losers, the French (hence the Marshal Soult incident with the "Napoleon" cask). When the French lost the war, he was execrated and boycotted in Jerez. The Domecqs, who had gradually infiltrated the business, and who had been more prudent politically, took over the firm.

It was at this point that the business genius, essential at some point in the success of every great firm, appeared, in the person of Pedro Domecq. He reorganised the entire business, modernised it on lines he had learnt in Bordeaux, supervising every detail in person, so that by 1825 it was the prinicpal sherry firm in Andalusia. It has never looked back. The secret of his success, he used to say, was his concentration on the English market. For after the Napoleonic wars, the most important man of fashion in Europe was the Prince Regent, who announced that he had had enough of French wine, and intended henceforth to drink sherry. As Jose-Ignazio Domecq said to me, "After this, every gentleman in England had to have a decanter of sherry on his sideboard."

The other sherry magnate whom I was fortunate enough to meet while I was in Jerez was the Marquis of Bonanza, otherwise known as Manolo Gonzalez, head of Gonzalez Byas. Aged eighty-six, his immense energy remains undiminished after a life of travel far and wide all over the globe selling his wares, and a sporting career similar to that of José-Ignazio Domecq. Tall, extremely affable and full of humour, he said, "I suppose you're fed up with hearing about sherry and polo, as if they were man and wife. But I'm afraid if you want to know anything about our firm, you've got to stomach a bit more. My grandfather introduced polo into Spain. He got it from England, and England got it from India. The Indians got it from Persia. And we gave it to the Argentines. And now they beat the lot of us. Now let's talk about sherry." And he showed me under a glass-topped table in his office these verses in English:

> I must have a drink at eleven,
> It's a duty that must be done;
> If I don't have a drink at eleven,
> Then I must have eleven at one.

The Marquis of Bonanza is regarded today as the father figure of the sherry trade, and he is affectionately known to everyone in the town as "Uncle Manolo" (Tio Manolo; "Just," he said, "like Tio Pepe, which we make. He was an earlier Uncle"). He told me that his firm was proud of its connection with England, but that one of their problems had always been to adapt themselves to the frequent changes in the kind of sherry demanded in England. "So constant have been the changes of taste," he said, "so endless the varieties, that we say there are as many types of sherry as there are shades of ribbon in a haberdasher's shop. At one time, a deep coloured, heavy wine will be in demand. At another, a wine paler in colour and lighter in body, but richer in flavour. Sometimes dry wines are in fashion; then comes the fashion for thin wines of a light tawny tint."

He told me, too, that as an Englishman I would be interested to hear of a curious connection between his firm and Lord Nelson. Jerez is only twenty miles from Cape Trafalgar, and it appears that after the battle, there was some question of Nelson's body being buried at sea – the normal procedure in those days for sailors fallen in battle. But in the case of so eminent a hero, it was decided to embalm his corpse and take it home for apotheosis in Westminster Abbey. The method employed for preserving in those days was to use alcohol; and Nelson's body was brought home to England in a vat of sherry.*

When I went round the bodegas, I was interested to see that Gonzalez Byas too, like Domecq, are in the habit of giving their butts the names of illustrious persons. But here, one might even say, they have gone one better than Domecq. Instead of military heroes, they have selected religious personalities which, in a devout land, is presumably an even better form of publicity. In their display bodega I saw twelve mammoth casks. "They are the Twelve Apostles," I was told by my guide. "You must drink from each of them." On the side of each I saw written the names of one of the Apostles: Matthew, Mark, Luke and John, down to Judas (from whose butt they advised me not to drink). But this was not

*It is said that when it was opened in London, all the sherry had been drunk.

all. These twelve butts are ranged six on each side of an even bigger, a gigantic cask, of Heidelberg proportions, which contains 3,000 gallons of sherry, with carved bunches of grapes and vine leaves on its sides. "This," he said, "is Christ."

The Marquis of Bonanza told me that his firm was founded by a young Manuel Gonzalez, of a noble but impoverished Madrid family which had found favour with the King, and been given the post of director of the salt marshes north of the nearby Quadalquiver. His father married the daughter of a well known local family. All went well until he died young, and his widow was left to bring up four sons. "This remarkable woman," he said, "to whom we owe our beginnings, had invested her very small capital in potatoes. The whole cargo of her potato crop, which represented all her wealth, was being ferried over the river to be sold on the north bank when the boat capsized and sunk. It seemed that all was lost. But she said, 'No! Potatoes float. We'll get another boat and pick them up.' No one took much notice of this, saying that the potatoes would sink. But she carried out her plan. They *did* float. She spent 48 hours in a hired boat picking up every potato – and thereby saved the family patrimony."

This small capital enabled her sons to start up in their various careers. Manuel Gonzalez, the youngest, unlike his elder brothers who were healthy and clever, was delicate and a poor student. He seemed to have little prospect in life and was articled as a clerk in a Cadiz firm. The stroke of luck necessary for success came with his marriage to the daughter of one of the richest families in Cadiz, the de Sotes (much against the will of that family). He abandoned his clerkship and set up in a modest way as a sherry shipper in Jerez. He made his first shipments to England in 1835, only ten butts, but by hard work and assisted by his wife's money, he had increased this within five years a hundred fold. By 1850 he was exporting 3,000 butts to England, and he decided to take an English partner into the firm, in the person of Robert Byass.

An important element in Gonzalez's sales propaganda is the cultivation of royal clients. They entertained Isabella II of Spain, and later Alfonso XII and his Queen, all of whom dedicated butts and left glowing testimonials, now framed and hanging on the office walls. To entertain Alfonso they hired the great French engineers, Eiffel, to design an elaborate oval *bodega*, the Concha, "half Albert Hall, half Crystal Palace" (as Rupert Croft-Cooke describes it in his informative book on sherry). The firm went from strength to strength in the late nineteenth century, the Byasses all being educated at Eton and Brasenose, while the two sons of Manuel Gonzalez were both ennobled by Alfonso XII, Manuel becoming Marquis of Bonanza, and Pedro, Marquis of Torre Soto de Brivesca. In modern times Alfonso XIII became a great friend of the family, often mounting their ponies in the polo field. The firm today has thousands of acres of vineyards surrounding the town of Jerez, and a stock of some thirty thousand butts. It is the biggest employer of labour in any of the world's winelands, and holds warrants from most of the remaining Royal houses.

Jerez has the best climate in Europe for the grape, its citizens claim, exactly 294 days a year of broiling sunshine, and exactly 71 days of rain. A "Vintage Year" as known in France and Oporto does not exist here, because all vintages are the same, all equally good, in both quantity and quality. This tendency, to take the weather for granted, is sometimes supplemented by a curious apathy about even one's own personal possessions. A certain Marquis who possesses some of the finest vineyards in Andalusia was dining one day in Madrid at the British Embassy, where he congratulated the British Ambassador on the excellence of his wine. "Where do you get stuff as good as this in Spain?" he asked "I'd like to buy some." The British Ambassador told him it came from the Marquis's own vineyard.

Baron Ricasoli
"The Father of the Italian Wine Industry"

As we go back in time, searching in the past for the commercial ancestors of the contemporary "Princes", we find that they become less distinct with each receding century. During the last one hundred and fifty years they are conspicuous enough; but by the Middle Ages, when the Church was the principal vineyard owner, the personalities, with the exception of such popes as Clement V, seem more symbolic than real.

However, there is no shortage of personalities in the nineteenth century, who are similar to our contemporary "Princes", for they too were primarily commercial men – indeed, they were the first to introduce the commercial methods of selling wine which we use today. Before these nineteenth-century men came on the scene, the methods of producing and marketing wine were still virtually mediaeval. Typical of these "new men" of the nineteenth century, who revolutionised the viticulture of his country, was the Tuscan, Baron Bettino Ricasoli; he has earned for himself the title "Father of the Italian wine industry".

The vine grows as luxuriantly in Italy as it does in Spain where, we have seen, the grapes are to be had almost for the picking. Not for nothing did the ancient Greeks name the Italian peninsula *"Eonotria"* ("The Wine Land") long before the name "Italy" was coined. Virgil, the professional husbandman of *The Georgics*, is almost lackadaisical about the care of vines, recommending that they should be draped about any upright that happens to be handy. And indeed in southern Italy they climb almost unaided by man. In Calabria, I once saw them clinging to a wayside crucifix – a

97

kind of macabre symbol of Life embracing Death, the delicate green tendrils entwining the legs of the Saviour.

One effect of this climatic exuberance in a land where "a bad year" is almost unknown, is that the vineyard owners have, throughout the centuries before Baron Bettino Ricasoli (1809–1880), neglected their vineyards and the careful pruning required for good wine. The result was that there was in Italy nothing of quality, only vast quantities of *vino nostrano*. Yet these Italian owners, the great landlords down the centuries, have had a longer wine history than most of the other European "Princes of the Grape". Some of them – the Corsinis, Capponis, Antinonis, Castelbarcos – have been making wine for six or seven hundred years, but almost exclusively for local consumption. Viticulture has been only one of the activities of these great Tuscan families, whose members have distinguished themselves by other activities, political and commercial. There is little therefore that the researcher can discover here about Italian "Princes of the Grape" with strongly defined characters – save in the case of the Ricasolis. It is not until the nineteenth century that one of them appears, the Baron Bettino Ricasoli, thanks to whom foreign markets were opened up with modern sales methods, so that for the first time in history an important new source of national revenue was tapped in Italy.

Most of these noble Florentine families trace their origins to the counting-house; but the Ricasolis have always been warriors, who regard bankers, like the Medicis, as upstarts. When these new rich were all arrogating to themselves titles to duchies and marquisates, the Ricasolis prided themselves on their relatively lowly estate of "baron". In the course of history they could have acquired many more grandiose titles but – to quote the family historian, Passerini – "they were more satisfied with the pride of being the only Barons of Tuscany than with becoming Counts and Earls Palatine, the latter often equal in conditions to many houses of the most vulgar origin."

Bettino Ricasoli, with whom we are concerned, is the most outstanding member of the family in modern times, known to history as the second prime minister of united Italy, and the successor of

Cavour in 1862. Although his considerable political achievements do not concern us here, one of the reasons why he strove so ardently for the union of Italy is closely connected with the wine trade. He foresaw that as long as Italy remained divided into a number of small states, it would be impossible to make industry efficient and competitive abroad, in particular the wine industry. This, he realised, was Italy's greatest potential source of wealth.

The family property at Brolio, which he inherited in 1832 with its vast acreage of vineyards was then typical of Italian viticulture; run on the most primitive lines, it had hardly changed for five hundred years. In an almost entirely agricultural country like Italy, life was easy for the hereditary landlords. They drank their native wines, and on the hot summer afternoons entertained one another with iced water-melon in the shady gardens of their villas, or in the courtyards of their cool *palazzi*. They left the running of their estates to the Factors, and were absentees most of the year, living on their considerable wine incomes in Rome, Florence or on the Riviera. Their interest in their workers extended little beyond half the produce which, under the 1,000 year-old *mezzadria* system the peasant had to furnish to his landlord. The peasant for his part, left to his own devices, became concerned only with the greatest immediate return from his plot, exhausting its wealth with his primitive assaults on its productivity. It did not occur to him that money might come from anything other than producing coarse wine and fattening pigs.

This was the situation at Brolio in southern Tuscany when Bettino Ricasoli inherited it from his lackadaisical father at the age of twenty-six. He was a different type of man, however. He had already acquired a considerable knowledge of the natural sciences, and his numerous notebooks reveal how he intended using this in the technical side of farm management. They refer to modern machinery, recipes for making *vino aleatico*, the proper nourishment and custody of cattle, etc. Such was his enthusiasm for science that he founded at Brolio a Museum of Natural History, with collections of minerals, shells, fossilised bones, skeletons, insects, marine products, plants, and a chemical laboratory. He then set about modernising his estate, taking up, unlike his peers, permanent residence on it with his family.

At first his wife objected to this; like all women of her class, she was accustomed to spending most of the year in Florence or Rome enjoying the social round. But he insisted – with the result that rumours soon circulated that she had a lover in Florence, and that Bettino Ricasoli was a kind of mediaeval ogre who had dragged his gentle lady off to imprisonment in his mountain fortress. Magnificent as it is Brolio is certainly a forbidding place, a mediaeval castle which has undergone more sieges than any other fortified *castello* in Tuscany, remote, in those days without proper roads, from all human habitation. His wife and daughter must have found the long winters there unbearably dull.

He now began his series of viticultural reforms, introducing the new methods he had closely studied on his visits abroad, in Bordeaux, Burgundy and the Rhineland. At first, he had some difficulty in changing the peasant's immemorial attitude to the vine. The careful pruning without which, Ricasoli had seen abroad, no good wine can be made, seemed to them an unnecessary labour. Accordingly, among the fifty-five peasant families living on his vineyards, Ricasoli imposed a strict discipline. Every evening he wrote out for his Factors instructions for the next day, all of which he saw carried out with his own eyes. Daily, whatever the weather, he toured his property, speaking to the peasants individually, learning their names. They soon realised that he knew more about wine-making than the Factors. If he found a viticultural practice of which he disapproved, the peasant was penalised. He drew up the *Regolamento agrario della Fattoria di Brolio*, in which every agricultural operation, from the pruning of the vines to the collection and disposal of manure, was described in detail. Every member of his staff had to have a copy, and every peasant had to read it or, if he could not read, have it read to him. For better management, he divided the wine production of his considerable property into five *fattorie* : at Brolio, Castagnoli, Meleto, Cacchiano and San Polo. The accounting he revised on the French model.

Although severe with his peasants, Ricasoli would hear nothing against them. "It is not the peasant's fault," he wrote, "that he is ignorant and uneducated – it is the landlord's. The peasant lacks the opportunity rather than the will. The landowner should never blame him – for the landlord either stays away from his estate altogether, or visits it only for the *uneducated* (italics author's) pleasure of the chase or the shoot." Moreover it was the duty of the landowner, he said, to care for the moral as well as the physical welfare of his peasants; he told them to regard him as a father rather than as a master. This again was something quite new in agrarian Italy, for the landlords had always considered that the peasant's moral requirements could be supplied perfectly adequately by the priest (who was often only a degree more literate than his charges).

Ricasoli introduced in the castle at Brolio a series of education courses for the peasants and their children. He put his wife and daughter in charge of a kind of Sunday School, to teach the young how to read and write, while he himself instructed the adults in religion and ethics. He was a kind of Italian Dr Arnold. A deeply devout man, he described and commented on the life of Christ and the Holy Scriptures. He told the peasants that agriculture was a God-given gift to man, "the purest, most beneficent and noble of all human activities", and that the agricultural worker was "the divine repository of the works of his Creator". He lectured them on the vice of idleness, showing that one hour lost by it every day represented three working days a month, or thirty in a year. Quoting from the Gospels, he showed them that man was born for the good of his fellow-men, and that even a poor man could find consolation in helping others. To his friend, the scientist Vieusseus, he wrote, "My friend, Tuscan agriculture needs heart as well as head. To me this work is an apostolate. Every Tuscan proprietor must be a born missionary."

Ricasoli's voluminous diaries and private papers give little indication of how the peasants responded to these lofty ideas. But their pay under his new system, benefiting from foreign sales, was greatly increased. We may assume therefore that they were content to work for a man who combined in his person the qualities of a mediaeval Baron, an evangelist preacher and a modern man of business.

Right up to the end in 1880, Bettino Ricasoli was still travelling widely in other wine-lands, to keep informed about the latest French and German methods. He even acquired vine shoots from as far away as the Canaries to improve his production; he was as erudite about wine-making in Portugal, Hungary or the Rheingau as in France and Italy. He opened markets for Italian wine in London and Paris, cities which had hardly ever heard of it. His pioneer work as a viticulturist was rewarded by the Italian state, and he was elected to the Academy of the Georgofili, most distinguished of Italian scientific bodies.

Ricasoli's political career is of interest to us here only in so far as it throws further light on his agricultural, and in particular viticultural, achievements. A great Italian patriot, he believed that Italy should be united, and the foreigners who controlled large provinces in it, in particular the Austrians, should be expelled. One method for aiding this process was to make Italy economically sound, not dependent on these foreigners. And here, in a land entirely without industry, in agriculture lay, he believed, the best prospect of success. Of all forms of agriculture, viticulture was the one which, owing to the sunny climate of the land, was most likely to benefit Italy.

In 1847, he accordingly founded a journal La Patria, and sent to the Grand Duke of Tuscany a memorial suggesting how agriculture could be improved. For this, a year later he was made Tuscan Minister of the Interior; here, he was primarily instrumental in promoting the union of Tuscany with Piedmont. For this achievement he was judged the best man to succeed Cavour in the premiership. As Premier he admitted the Garibaldian volunteers to the regular army, revoked the decree of exile against Mazzini, and attempted reconciliation with the Vatican. But his efforts were rendered ineffectual by the Pope's non possumus, and he had to resign.

He returned to Brolio to take up his old work, reflecting that the managing of an estate was as exacting and difficult as the government of a nation. One maxim, he said, applied as much to a landlord as to a prime minister: "Do good for the people who are entrusted to your care." He now reverted to the habits of his early days at Brolio. His daughter had died, but she had left him two grandchildren whom he adored, and whom he educated with the aid of maps, books and scientific devices. He began work every morning at 4 am, and went to bed before nine in the evening. The mornings he spent at his desk; and in the afternoon, whether under the blazing summer sun of central Italy or the rains and ruins of January, he was astride his horse, riding round his estate. As Mr Hancock says in his excellent biography: "To the peasants, it seemed as if he had never left them. They knew he had become great in the world, for they had seen the King himself come to Brolio to do him honour." Now as in the early days, he encouraged them, led them, ordered them, chided them. They were told to be pious, industrious, thrifty and clean; they must be up early, teach their children the Commandments and the Scriptures, they must love their wives, love God and Italy. He died at Brolio on 23 October 1880. His private life and public career had been marked by such austerity that he has come to be known as the "Iron Baron".

When I visited Brolio in September 1973, I was taken there from Florence by his descendant, the present Baron (also called Bettino), in the company of a group of English wine-merchants. He had hired a bus and we trundled along, some thirty strong, for two hours through the beautiful rolling Tuscan landscape, while he described some of the present problems of Chianti wine.

In this slim figure, youthful for his fifty years, with a restrained, almost retiring manner and a spontaneous courtesy to all and sundry, it may be hard at first to see the direct descendant of those mighty paladins of feudal times who dominated Tuscany by force of arms – even of the dynamic "Iron Baron", his grandfather. But as he talked on, one became increasingly aware of his force of character. He it was who, by his undaunted efforts, was primarily responsible for the present proper classification of Italian wine in Tuscany. Until the Second World War, everyone who made wine in Tuscany called it "Chianti" – a name of world renown, which promoted sales. But the quality varied greatly; only in a restricted area running north from Siena were the grapes of the highest quality. "The reputation," he explained, "of our first quality wine in this area was being brought into disrepute by inferior stuff bearing the same name. So we fought with the state authorities to get the wine from the first quality given the exclusive right to call itself 'Chianti Classico'. It was a struggle – but now everyone knows that when he has a bottle with simply 'Chianti' on it, it is an inferior wine. The good wine is always marked 'Chianti Classico' – from these vineyards." He was standing with us on the battlements of Brolio, his feudal castle, looking out over the sea of rolling vineyard below, over the valley of the Arbia, where his ancestors had bloodily fought on a day fateful in the history of Florence, to the blue hills far away to the south and the great mass of Monte Amiata.

That this present Bettino Ricasoli should take such trouble to accompany personally a small group of relatively unimportant British wine-merchants and persons like myself from Florence to Brolio at his own expense, to spend hours taking us round his cellars describing them and the wine processes, to act as host at an excellent lunch, is surely a sign, not only that he is a worthy descendant of his great forbear, but of the times. Not only is he fully conversant with every phase of wine-making, all of which he supervises himself, but he is clearly aware that in impoverished Europe today, the work is too important to be left to the factors (if he has any). Every year, too, he travels to the USA with a group of international vintners, lecturing all over the continent on viticulture, and finding markets for his wares. The great nineteenth century Bettino Ricasoli would surely be proud of this descendant who bears his Christian name.

Recently, thanks largely to the efforts of Ricasoli, Tuscan wines have found a growing market in England. Here they are supported in a remarkable way today by an English family who have been making wine in Tuscany for most of this century, the Sitwells of Renishaw, who owned the famous vineyard of Montegufoni near Florence. Mr Reresby Sitwell, having sold Montegufoni and wishing to continue the family wine tradition with Tuscany, has transferred Montegufoni vines to his Renishaw estate in Yorkshire, where his first vintage is being produced this year (1975).

II

Ingham and Woodhouse in Marsala

The other great nineteenth-century innovator in the Italian wine industry was a Yorkshireman, Benjamin Ingham, who spent most of his life in Marsala, where he was finally created a Sicilian baron. He arrived in Sicily at the age of twenty-two, in 1806, with very little capital. When he died in 1861 his estate in Italy alone, founded on Marsala wine, was valued at £9,000,000.

The name Ingham has been fairly common in Yorkshire since the time of Charles I – inn-keepers, shop-keepers, school-teachers, sometimes house servants have borne it. By the opening of the nineteenth century, a branch had become prominent in the Leeds wool trade; and in 1806 this family sent the young Benjamin to Sicily to open a market in cloth. There is a legend that the youth, having been jilted by his fiancée, had vowed to abandon his native land, and not return to it until he could buy up the whole Yorkshire district where he was born.*

On arriving in Sicily, he quickly realised the potentialities of Marsala wine, which was becoming very popular in the British navy – then dominating Sicilian waters under Nelson. Napoleon had closed the continent to Britain, so that our fleet could not obtain its normal rations of madeira and rum. Thanks to Nelson's partiality for Marsala, it now replaced those beverages. Nelson wrote to his Commander-in-Chief, Lord Keith, "Marsala wine is so good that any gentleman's table might receive it; and it will be of real use to our seamen."

*See *Princes under the Volcano* by Raleigh Trevelyan, an excellent account of the life and times of English families in Sicily in the late eighteenth and early nineteenth centuries (Macmillan, 1972).

Although Ingham had come out to deal in "rags" (as the wool trade was called), he quickly turned to wine, and soon knew more about its production than did the natives, as his monograph for their benefit reveals: *Brief Instructions for the vintage with the object of improving the vines.* In this, he deals with precautions immemorially ignored by the Sicilians, such as holding the vines well away from the ground to eliminate the earthy taste. He recommends that the vintage should be carried out in two operations not, as previously, in one, so that the mature grapes are not thrown in with the bitter ones. He also gives detailed information for the scientific fermentation of the must.

He and his predecessor by two decades, John Woodhouse – a lesser man whose career is described later in this chapter – inaugurated what proved to be an agrarian revolution in Sicily. When they arrived, the cultivation of the vine was limited, because the indigent local population found the olive and the sumach (for tanning) more lucrative. The Englishmen changed all this. They offered loans to farmers to clear their olive groves and wheat fields, and to plant vines instead. They invested capital to develop these vineyards, and bought the grape juice at a price they fixed themselves. They paved the main street of Marsala – until then a dirt track – and built a jetty and harbour for the shallow draught sailing ships which carried their wines to England. (The jetty was the one on which Garibaldi and his Thousand were to land in 1860.) They epitomised the remark made by a Sicilian about his island as late as 1840, "Few Sicilians carry on commerce with much energy; the greater part of the profits in wine spring from the activity of foreigners."

Ingham was also a social innovator, if that term can be applied in the context of the British colony in Sicily. For until he arrived the British merchants mixed very little with the natives, nor did they bother to learn Italian; they all intermarried. Benjamin Ingham broke with this habit. He learnt Italian, even taking the trouble to master the difficult Sicilian dialect. He also took an Italian mistress, the widowed Duchess of Santa Rosalia, who seems to have been attracted by the great sales of wine which this rough Englishman had so swiftly achieved. Thanks to the liaison, he became the only member of the English trading community to mix on more or less equal terms with the Sicilian grandees. They, for their part, had no objection to the foreign upstart living with one of their members so long as he provided them with loans when they were in debt – a perennial state.

He later married his Duchess, which further enhanced his social standing. We find him and his wife in 1828 entertaining the Duke of Buckingham who had arrived in his yacht, and was much fêted by the Sicilian Grandees. Ingham entertained his noble countryman lavishly; but characteristically he regarded the money spent as a sound investment, for he later wrote, "The noble Lord insisted on paying five times the value of our collection of Greek vases."

Ingham's remarkable contribution to the prosperity of the island, not only by expanding a hundred fold its Marsala wine business with England and America, but by investing in a number of depressed local industries such as flax and shipping, earned for him in 1840 the thanks of a grateful monarch: he was created Baron Ingham of the Kingdom of the Two Sicilies.

The nineteenth century was the heyday of the family firm and Ingham felt, like most of his contemporaries, that the surest business associates were those linked by ties of blood. As the business grew he needed help. He therefore summoned from England his four nephews: Joshua and Benjamin Ingham junior, sons of his brother Joseph; and the two Whitaker boys, sons of his sister Mary. They did not all come out at once, but as Ingham required them. Thus, when the elder Whitaker boy, who worked for him in Marsala, died prematurely, Ingham wrote characteristically to his sister, Mary Whitaker, "Your son is dead. Send me another." The "other" was the famous Joseph Whitaker who was to become a mainstay of the firm. A born accountant, he was never happier than when sitting at his desk totting up figures, watching over his uncle's wealth with an eagle eye. And well he might have, for it was later all to come to his descendants.

Ingham needed someone reliable in the office, because in the 1830s and 1840s he was often abroad, chiefly in America, having foreseen the growing importance of the American market. Here he was particularly ingenious. Trade between the United States and Sicily at this time was very one-sided. The only American exports to pay for wine were the barrel staves for the Sicilian cooperage. But this corresponded to only a small part of the American wine imports; Sicilian wine merchants like Ingham found they were building up large credits in the States, which could be transferred only by way of London, at a considerable discount. Ingham refused to do this, preferring to take the risk and invest his dollars in the newly laid American railroads. As we know now, these railroads made fortunes for anyone who "got in on the ground floor". By 1860, Ingham was registered as owning forty per cent of the New York Central railroad stock. He also had $100,000 in the St Mary Falls Ship Canal Company. He owned land in Manhattan, including a part of what is now Fifth Avenue. He also bought land on the outskirts of the rapidly expanding city of New York, at agricultural prices – which he retained until he sold it at building prices.

When Ingham died in 1861, there was some speculation as to whom he would leave his vast fortune. Because the Ingham nephews were childless, the most likely benefactor seemed Joseph Whitaker's eldest son Benjamin; but to everyone's surprise Ingham left to the younger son William, a sum which, together with the American assets, amounted to over ten million pounds.

This partiality for William Whitaker is explained by a curious legend, still related in the family; it is perfectly in keeping with Ingham's dour Yorkshire character. He had originally favoured the elder son, Benjamin, his namesake; but a small and apparently insignificant incident changed his mind. One day, he learnt that these two Whitaker brothers had gone for a country walk, which at one point involved crossing a toll-bridge. Benjamin reached the destination first, because he paid the 2d toll charge. But William, rather than pay, preferred to make the long detour of three miles to reach the destination. Such "penny-wise" philosophy made an immediate appeal to Benjamin Ingham, who promptly altered his will in favour of the younger brother.

As so often happens in the case of inherited wealth, William

Whitaker and his heirs soon lost interest in the source of their fortune. One branch of the family returned to England, where they bought the extensive property and grounds of Pylewell Park near Southampton, and cultivated exotic plants in the relaxing air of the Solent. The other branch, under the influence of three socially ambitious women who had married Whitakers, became the rulers of Palermitan society, entertaining a host of celebrities at their palatial villa Malfitano outside Palermo. George V, Queen Mary and Prince George lunched there in 1925, and the King then personally conducted the Whitakers over the royal yacht. On another occasion they entertained the German Kaiser. G. M. Trevelyan on a visit to Sicily about this time wrote of Whitaker's wife, Tina, "The wife of a very wealthy English Marsala wine merchant, but *née* the daughter of a very poor Sicilian exile in the Fifties ... the daughter of a Republican revolutionary, she now hobnobs with Royalty." In the summer months, these Whitakers wandered round northern Europe staying with friends, accompanied by a retinue of nurses, governesses, valets and ladies' maids. In London they were visited at Claridge's by the Empress Eugénie, Lady Warwick, Mrs Ronnie Greville, Princess Marie-Louise, the Duke and Duchess of Schleswig-Holstein. When Joseph Whitaker died in 1933, *The Times* wrote in its obituary, "There was probably no house in Europe where one met such distinguished and cosmopolitan society as at Malfitano." Such were the social fruits of a fortune made from Marsala wine by a humble Yorkshire trader who had come out to Sicily in 1806.

The other important, if lesser, figure in the Marsala trade was Ingham's predecessor and, in a sense, his mentor, John Woodhouse. He was responsible for the Nelson connection. Like Ingham, he came from the English northern commercial classes, being sent as a young man from Liverpool by his family to Sicily in 1770, to trade in barilla. Like Ingham a few decades later, he soon realised that traffic in Marsala wine was more lucrative; and he conceived the highly original idea (in those days) of going to Spain to learn how Malaga wine was made. He realised that both Malaga on the east coast of Spain, and Marsala in Sicily, are on the same latitude, and have a similar soil, a mixture of calcium sulphate and ferrous oxide which produced the same type of heavy, highly alcoholic wine. From Spain, he also borrowed the *solera* system – a cask of "mother wine" never more than half empty being continually topped up by new wine every time a quantity is drawn off.

By 1790 he was exporting 8,000 gallons of Marsala wine annually to Liverpool. The great popularity which this wine now gained in England was largely, we have already seen, due to Lord Nelson's partiality for it. Commanding the British fleet in Sicilian waters, Nelson was often at Palermo, where he took a liking to John Woodhouse, whom he invited aboard his flagship, the *Vanguard*. In the ship's inventory is an order from Nelson to Woodhouse for 200 pipes of Marsala for the British fleet.*

It may seem strange (comments Raleigh Trevelyan in his account of the English in Sicily at this time) that Nelson and Woodhouse should have become so friendly, for the two men could not have been more dissimilar. Woodhouse was an ascetic nonconformist whose only interest was in business; he could hardly have approved of the irregular life led by Nelson when not at sea. For at the end of 1798, Nelson took Sir William and Lady Hamilton on board the *Vanguard*, and they made their famous escape from Naples to Palermo, where the *ménage à trois* began. During 1799, Nelson and Emma Hamilton were fêted royally in Palermo by the Sicilian grandees, in an unending succession of balls, masquerades, dinners, concerts and all-night sessions of faro.

John Woodhouse often had to visit Palermo at this time, to maintain the wine connection with the British Navy. He attempted to avoid these festivities, but they were forced on him because he had to put up at the only habitable hotel in the town, where a number of Lady Hamilton's friends were lodged. He was much offended by their immoral behaviour. However, he evidently did not announce his disapproval publicly, because we find Nelson writing on 20 March to his Commander-in-Chief, "I have agreed with Woodhouse of Marsala for 500 pipes of wines to be delivered to our ships at Malta, at 1s 5d per gallon. As Mr Woodhouse runs

*A pipe is a barrel holding 105 gallons.

all the risks, pays all the freight, etc, I don't think it's a bad bargain." Such was the excellence of one particular brand of Woodhouse's Marsala that Nelson gave him permission to call it Bronte Marsala (as it is known today).* That Marsala became very popular with the British sailors is attested by a picture which used to hang in the Woodhouse *baglio* (warehouse) at Marsala showing French prisoners-of-war enjoying their tots of it aboard a British warship after Trafalgar.

We have already seen the benefits, commercial and social, which Woodhouse (in conjunction with Ingham) had brought to the island. Woodhouse was also noted for his charitable works. During a famine, he imported grain for the population at his own expense. Such was his reputation for good works, as well as integrity, that he was never molested by the Mafia. Until the end of his life, he was able to drive unescorted and unarmed in a countryside infested with bandits, with a box at the back of his cart containing the money for paying the growers.

With the decline of the Marsala trade at the end of the nineteenth century, the Woodhouses suffered much the same fate as did Ingham's firm. Neither of the last two Woodhouse brothers had much flair for business. They preferred hunting and shooting to the office stool, and let the firm fall into the hands of a corrupt maternal uncle called Harvey. He is said to have deliberately let the firm run down, so that he might buy it cheap from his nephews. He was a red head, of whom it was said in Palermo, "He was more interested in social life and the ladies, as witness the number of red heads now scattered all over the island." After his death, the firm was run nominally by another nephew, Frederick Woodhouse, but he too soon lost interest; and the firm was wound up in the early twentieth century.

---

*Nelson had also helped the Bourbon Royal family to escape, for which the grateful King Ferdinand created him Duke of Bronte and a Grandee of Sicily.

12

Aristocrats in Germany

In the Latin lands bordering the Mediterranean plenty of *vin ordinaire* as well as fine wine, is produced. In France, Italy and Spain, wine is the normal beverage of the populace, who imbibe it at every meal almost as freely as water. In these countries, therefore, there is always a market for cheap wine, and the vintners cater for it accordingly; only twenty per cent of the wine in France is *Appellation Contrôlée*. But across the eastern frontiers of France, in the principal wine-growing region of Germany, along the banks of the river Rhine and its tributaries, drinking habits are very different.

Here wine has never been the staple drink. The German peasant and poorer classes have, like the English proletariat, always preferred beer; when they drink wine, it has been for some solemn or festive occasion, for which they are prepared to pay relatively high prices. The result of this is that down the ages the great vine-growing capacity of the Rhine and its tributaries, the Mosel, the Main and the Nahe, have been adapted to a different clientele, to producing exclusively high quality wine for the rich and mighty of this world. It is no coincidence that so many of the great Rhenish vine owners for centuries, down to our own times, have feudal names – Graf Matuschka-Greiffenclau, the Grafen von und zu Eltz, the Fürst von Metternich, Graf von Francken-Sierstorpf, Prince Friedrich Heinrich of Prussia. These men and many others are still producing wine from vineyards which have been in their families for as long as seven centuries (for example, Schloss Vollrads of the Matuschka-Greiffenclaus). Thus, wine growing in Germany has been until quite modern times an essentially aristocratic activity. Only in the last century has the *négociant* appeared on the scene (whom we have already seen active in France since the mid-seventeenth century), sitting in his office in Frankfurt or Mainz.

This distinction between Mediterranean and German viticulture is also seen in the attitudes adopted by the respective vintners. Whereas the vineyards in France tend to be the principal interest of their owners, to which they devote all their working hours, in search of profit, to the owners in Germany the vineyards have been only one of many interests. The mediaeval German nobleman was, almost by definition, concerned exclusively with the acquisition and exercise of power, in particular political power; his varied possessions and fiefs all contributed to this aim; among them, only one of many, was his vineyard. This served two purposes only – to provide wine for his table, and to obtain political favours: to bribe his superiors, the cardinal archbishop, the elector, even the Kaiser himself. His wine therefore had to be of superlative quality; for the great and powerful of this world, even if they cannot always recognise a good picture or a good poem, are quick to savour the material things of life, food, drink, pleasure and comfort, and to condemn them if they are inferior. The German vineyard owners therefore concentrated on a small output, but of the highest quality. That it was not a commercial proposition did not worry them; it was a *political* proposition, amply repaying their expenditure in other ways.

Remnants of this feudal attitude lingered on in Germany until as late as the early nineteenth century. Until 1805, with the arrival of Napoleon, the Eltzs at Eltville, for example, had a seigniorial right to exact a duty on every barge carrying wine which passed a certain point of the Rhine. Napoleon abrogated this right. But after his fall in 1815 when conditions returned to normal (or so the German seigneurs hoped), the Eltzs demanded a restitution of their ancestral dues. But the situation had irremediably changed since the French Revolution, and they had to present their case to the *Reichshofgericht*, for which legal representation was necessary. For nearly fifty years they were engaged in this litigation, employing a series of lawyers, always to no avail.

It was not until 1865 that, realising that only the lawyers were benefiting, they abandoned the claim. In viticultural terms this date in the mid-nineteenth century may be said to mark the end of feudal wine owning habits in Germany; it is now that the *négociants* appear in the Rhineland, nearly two hundred years after their arrival in France and Portugal.

For most of the aristocrats the Rhenish vineyards were only a part of their property. The Eltzs had other vineyards in the Mosel and Croatia (where they introduced the Riesling grape); the Metternichs had winelands in Bohemia, and the Greiffenclaus, large properties in Franconia. A number of these lands were lost after the Second World War when the communist régimes in those countries sequestrated them. In the long run the loss of these lands in Bohemia and Croatia benefited the vineyards in the Rhineland because, being all that remained to the owners who now found themselves pressed for money, they now had a personal interest taken in their cultivation. The inherited wealth of their owners was now severely taxed; the great owners could no longer treat their Rhenish vineyards as luxuries producing largesse for the tables of their friends and patrons. They had to make them commercial concerns.

No vintners can ever have had a more discouraging or difficult task than the Germans – poor soil, short summers, lack of sunshine and precipitous slopes to be terraced. But thanks to the famous German *Fleiss* their labourers triumphed magnificently over Nature. Her handicaps seem only to have spurred these undaunted men onto greater efforts and viticultural discoveries.

The best known Rheingau vineyard is Schloss Johannisberg, principally because its owner, after 1815, was the Austrian Chancellor, Prince Clemens von Metternich of Congress of Vienna fame, and it has remained in his family ever since. To the average non-German, the association of an Austrian statesman in Vienna with a distant vineyard, three-quarters of the way up the Rhine, seems singular. In fact, the Austrian Chancellor was not an Austrian but a Rhinelander, born at Koblenz, whose family had always held important government posts in the various Rhenish Electorates. From the Middle Ages down to relatively modern times, the

Rhineland has furnished, like all parts of what we today call Germany, "Electors", each of whom had a vote in the election of every new Holy Roman Emperor. Gradually the seat of this empire had become established in Vienna (in the fourteenth and fifteenth centuries it was in Prague). The Rhineland provided three Electors, the Prince Bishops of respectively Cologne, Mainz and Trier. While primarily concerned with ruling their own provinces, these men always looked to Vienna, the fount of power. Their relations and liegemen did the same, tending to gravitate to Vienna, where they would have considerable standing because of their connections with the Elector. It was an age of nepotism.

Such was the case with Clemens von Metternich, later the great Austrian Chancellor. His father was a diplomat who had passed from the service of the Bishop Elector of Trier to that of the court of Vienna. The son did the same, becoming the greatest statesman of his age. It was in return for his services, culminating in the Congress of Vienna, that the Austrian Emperor made him a prince and bestowed on him Johannisberg, which had become after 1815 an imperial fief. In view of Metternich's local origins, therefore, the association of Austrian Chancellor and Rhenish vineyard may seem less singular.

In the words of Francis II's "Donation": "For Our faithful servant von Metternich and his male heirs, in gratitude for services rendered to the State in the last period of the European wars, for establishing the peace – a lasting monument of our pleasure and gratitude." That this "lasting monument" rejoiced the heart of Chancellor Metternich is to be seen in a letter he wrote to his wife shortly after taking possession of Johannisberg in the autumn of 1818:

> From the balcony of Johannisberg I can see the course of the Rhine for twenty miles and open country beyond to the horizon. At least ten towns and countless villages lie before my gaze; and then the vast extent of the vineyard and the *Schlösser*, meadows and woodland; and nearby are fruit trees weighted down with their produce. What a landscape! What a breathtaking beauty for the newcomer to the Rheingau! Such

is the view on a clear day, the river alive with two-masted sailing ships. When it is misty the mighty Rhine seems to disappear into the distance, as if it were no longer a river, but part of a great sea. . . .

Before the irruption of the French revolutionary troops in 1800, Johannisberg and its vineyard belonged to a Benedictine monastery, whose chapel was dedicated to John the Baptist (hence its present name). After the Peace of Lunéville in 1801, when the French frontiers were advanced to the Rhine, Napoleon expelled the monks and offered the property to Prince William of Orange-Nassau, hoping thereby to enrol the Dutchman in his Rhine Confederacy. When Prince William refused both gift and recruitment, Napoleon bestowed it on his Marshal Kellermann, the victor of Valmy. But the upstart general did not enjoy it for long because, after Napoleon's fall in 1814, it passed to his principal adversary, the Emperor of Austria, who in turn gave it to Metternich.

The Imperial Donation contained a curious proviso. Every year Metternich and his descendants were to reserve one-tenth of the Johannisberg vintage for the Habsburg Emperor, to be paid to him and his descendants in perpetuity. This proviso was faithfully observed by the Metternichs, down to our own day, even after the fall of the Habsburg dynasty. In 1918 the new Austrian Republic attempted to appropriate the tithe, as a perquisite devolving on the Habsburgs' political successors; but the Metternichs successfully defended it as a contract made not with the Emperor as head of state, but with him as a private person. To this day, the tithe is paid to the Pretender to the throne of the Habsburgs, the Archduke Otto.

To maintain a franchise of this kind for over a hundred and fifty years may seem something of a supererogation – were it not for the commercial value of publicity in our times. Shakespeare may have been right in the sixteenth century when he said, "a good wine needs no bush"; but in the thrusting, highly competitive twentieth century it certainly needs one; and "the wine of Kings" is about as good a designation as any vintner could want.*

*The recent visit (1972) of the Prince of Wales to Johannisberg is in the same royal tradition.

Due largely to this royal connection, the name "Johannisberg" is better known today than that of almost any other wine in the world.

The Metternich who acquired Johannisberg in 1816 has the reputation of being one of the biggest reactionaries in history, accused of repressing liberty in Germany, Spain and Italy. He is also regarded as the epitome of the *ancien régime* statesman, with charm of manner, great social gifts, the ease and versatility with which he handled diplomatic questions, together with a certain reputation for gallantry and intrigue. All this may well be true, but in domestic affairs he was not the whole-hearted reactionary of popular imagination.

When he acquired Johannisberg he quickly revealed a business acumen which, for a German aristocrat of his time, must have seemed incongruous. He actually tried to make the vineyard pay – as some of the agreements he made with the new class of *négociants* appearing in the local cities reveal. On 30 June 1823, Metternich signed an agreement with M. A. Rothschild & Sons, Frankfurt-am-Main, in which his wines are classified in various categories, each with a different price (something unheard of in Germany before). In 1829, he signed an agreement with the firm of D. Leiden of Cologne referring to his first, second and third categories of wine, "because the different qualities are inadequately marked for the buyer by the different colour of the labels and seals". A significant observation on the changing scene is also revealed as early as 1825, in a letter to him from the *négociant*, Kiffer, who writes, "The wine you suggest for England at 15–20 gulden a bottle is too expensive – because Steinbergen is selling the same quality at 10 gulden." He adds, "We should not forget that the public is no longer looking for old wine in such quantities as formerly."

The apostle of reaction in politics certainly did not apply those principles in his commercial dealings. He took a personal part in the wine making and marketing. He selected the position for the new vines himself and supervised the cellar arrangements, in particular the type of bottles and their filling. He was careful in choosing his cellar-masters who ran the vineyard when he was away –

the monk Pater Arndt, and Johann Heckler. Of the latter he wrote, "I have selected this man because I know that over many years he has acquired a quite unusually extensive knowledge of viticulture, and a talent for experiment."

The other cellar-master, Pater Karl Arndt from Fulda, became his Dom Pérignon – except that his extraordinary flair for wine came from his nose and not his palate. Pater Arndt had such repugnance for drinking wine that, throughout his time at Johannisberg, he never touched a drop. And yet it was sufficient for him to scent the bouquet to know what year it was. "On no occasion," wrote Metternich to his wife, "has Pater Arndt ever been mistaken over this. Heaven has endowed him with this gift."

In 1841 he wrote, "Our wines have a great European reputation, which we must maintain and extend. What is not good enough to be bottled must be disposed of in other ways." His commercial sense is again revealed in his instructions that low quality wine was to be sold as soon as possible, while good wine was to be held. He was well aware that the rich man has the advantage over the poor, of being able to keep his wine until the most favourable moment for sale. By 1845 he was selling his wine through the *négociants* in Paris, London, Berlin, St Petersburg, Hanover and Leipzig – to such customers as the Queen of England, the Egyptian Bey, Prince Ismael, and the Archduke Michael of Russia.

His concern for quality and reliability at a time when adulteration was fairly common is revealed in another letter, of 30 June 1830. "Henceforth no bottled wine from Johannisberg is to be put on the market unless the labels are countersigned by the cellar-master. This measure is to be made known to the public through the Frankfurt newspaper *Oberspostamts-Zeitung*." This was the famous *Kabinetteswein Etikett* still in use today (the 1974 bottle labels of Johannisberg are all countersigned by "B. Labonte", the present cellar-master). He further ordered that only the Riesling grape was to be used, in preference to the cheaper but quantity yielding Sylvaner.*

*The Riesling-Sylvaner relationship can be compared with that of Pinot-Gamay in Burgundy – see chapter 14. Just as the Gamay, despised on

Further innovations introduced by the great Metternich were: the building of new houses for the vineyard workers and their families, and extra awards of 5, 10 and 15 gulden for the best workers; the *Weinausschenk* is still in use today, where the casual or passing visitor can visit the cellars and then sit out on the terrace with a free glass of wine admiring the view onto the Rhine and the distant Hunsrück range.

After his resignation as Chancellor during the 1848 troubles, and his exile in London, Metternich took up residence at Johannisberg where he was visited by most of the great of Europe, who seem to have enjoyed the wine as much as his company. Here he entertained Goethe and the young Bismarck, who had come to Frankfurt as the Prussian representative at the German Parliament. Metternich's wife wrote in her diary, "Bismarck is only thirty-six, but he already appears to have a sound basis of political thought. My husband was much struck by him, and says he has brilliance." In 1851, Metternich received the Prussian King, Friedrich Wilhelm IV, who landed by boat with his suite at the nearby Rhineside village of Geisenheim. Later the King wrote to Metternich, "I always thank God that you are back in Germany, at Johannisberg again – and that conditions are so very different from what they were only three years ago." The 1848 uprisings all over Europe had been crushed, largely through the system and measures associated with Metternich's name.

When he died on 11 June 1859, he left to his descendants a vineyard which was modern by the standards of the time, and whose name was now known far beyond the frontiers of Germany.

In AD 822 a chapel to St Nicholas, the patron saint and protector of the Rhineland shipping, was erected on the hillock now called Johannisberg. Charlemagne, the owner of many vineyards, observing that the snow melted earlier on the southern-facing slopes

---

the Côte d'Or, burgeons into glory in the Beaujolais, so does the Sylvaner, indifferent in the Rheingau, come into its own in Rhenish Hesse and the Palatinate.

of the Rheingau than elsewhere in northern Europe, directed that vineyards should be planted here. Two hundred years later, Johannisberg obtained its name when the Archbishop of Mainz founded the Benedictine monastery dedicated to St John the Baptist. A nunnery was also situated at the foot of the hill near the village of Geisenheim. These religious orders cultivated the grape assiduously for three hundred years and became extremely prosperous – so prosperous that by the fourteenth century, affluence had led to good living and dissipation (see Chapter 15, *The Vineyards of the Lord*). The nuns in particular appear to have got out of hand; they were ordered to leave by their bishop, and when they refused were excommunicated and expelled by force.

Meanwhile the monks must have continued making wine in Johannisberg, because in 1525 during the Peasants' Revolt the insurgents invaded the property and became so drunk in the cellars that they placidly allowed themselves to be arrested – having until then easily overthrown the forces of law and order. Nine of them were publicly hanged in Eltville.

The present cellars were built by the monks in 1721. The dark wine-coloured mushroom growth on the walls and ceilings contributes to the atmosphere which Rheingau wine requires for its peculiar steely bouquet. But it was not until 1775 that the greatest technical innovation in German wine production took place in Johannisberg.

The vineyard was now under the direct control of the Fulda Bishopric (Fulda is the Canterbury of the German Catholic Church), which gave instructions that the annual vintage was not to begin until the Archbishop's written permission was received. The vintage starts a little later here than in the rest of western Europe, in order to take advantage of every ray from the late autumn sun. The summer and autumn of 1775 were superb; early in October the mounted courier set off from Fulda with the permission for the vintage to begin. But for reasons which have never been discovered, he did not arrive at Johannisberg; either he fell ill and died on the way, or was waylaid by highwaymen. The monks of Johannisberg, contemplating their fat grapes maturing under the hot sun waited impatiently day by day, week by week. By the end of October, they saw that the grapes were beginning to rot on their stems, dried up by the uncommonly sunny days of that late October. When they at last sent their own courier to Fulda and obtained permission, it seemed too late. Nevertheless, they harvested the grapes which, shrivelled as they were, they pressed into wine. To their surprise, they found that they had produced one of the finest vintages ever known – small in quantity but unsurpassed in quality, with a subtle, non-sugary sweetness and a wonderful bouquet. This then was the origin of the term *Spätlese* (late picking), now used for the highest quality Rheingau wine, the grapes being allowed, in a good October, not only to over-ripen but to shrivel on their stems before gathering. If the good weather continues into November, and sometimes even into December before gathering, a *Trockenbeerenauslese*, is obtained, the greatest vintage of all.

After the death of the great Chancellor Metternich, both his son and grandson preferred to live on their large estates in Bohemia, and they left Johannisberg to the care of their cellar-masters. It was not until after the Second World War and the sequestration by the communists of their Bohemian property at Königsberg, that the present holder of the title, Prince Paul Metternich, made Johannisberg his home and devoted himself seriously to wine-making there. The Schloss and wineries had been almost completely destroyed by the RAF on the night of 13 August 1942; but German *Fleiss* again overcame all difficulties. Prince Paul and his cellar-master, Domänenrat Herr Labonte, rebuilt the Schloss and replanted the vines – so that today Johannisberg is producing more first-class wine than ever before in its history. Prince Paul has introduced the system of workers' participation in the direction of the firm, and each worker has been given a small plot of his own in the vineyard. In the intervals of running his vineyard Prince Paul Metternich is, like his counterpart in France, Baron Philippe de Rothschild, an accomplished racing motorist. He is President of the German Motor Racing Association.

Although the Metternichs are an Old Rhenish family their history, as vineyard owners, goes back no further than 1815 – which by Rheingau standards is not far. Many other German wine families can trace ownership for half a millennium. The oldest, the Grafen von Matuscha-Greiffenclau have owned Schloss Vollrads and its vineyards for seven hundred years. They are first referred to in the archives in this connection in 1211.

Their history is typical of most of the old viticultural families of the Rheingau, Rhenish Hesse and the Palatinate, the principal wine growing areas of Germany. Throughout the centuries their name is always cropping up among important dignitaries in church and state, with references to their gifts of wine to local and imperial potentates. When they first appear in 1211, we read of the two brothers, Emmircho and Heinrich Greiffenclau* who agreed to furnish "three cart-loads of Hunnish homegrown wine (sic) in return for a political concession".

Although owning Schloss Vollrads, the third biggest vineyard in the Rheingau, they appear generally to have been absentee landlords. When Goethe visited Schloss Vollrads in 1814 to see its famous art treasures, he found only a caretaker; the Greiffenclau owner was living on his estates in Franconia. Goethe describes the dilapidated condition of Schloss Vollrads:

> "The courtyard of the castle, which is encircled by dwelling houses and other outhouses of considerable size, bears witness to a state of prosperity in days gone by. . . . The interior presents a desolate appearance. Here all that remains are life-size portraits of innumerable ancestors, Electors, prebendaries and knights, hanging in this desolate though not entirely devastated hall where old, once luxurious furniture still stands. . . . If we turn our gaze from this disorder to the window, a most glorious view is obtained; the wild-looking but fruitful vineyard lies directly beneath, and through a gently widening valley, the town of Winkel is seen in its entire length, while beyond on the other side of the Rhine are the fertile districts of Lower and Upper Ingelheim. We walked through the neglected garden to

*The name is feudal, meaning "griffen's claw"–the emblem worn on their helmets and breastplates in battle and tourney.

the vineyards, and found them in the same forlorn condition. The owner, we were told, lives on his other estates far away, and is evidently not much interested in Vollrads and its wine. . . ."

We may think of Vollrads throughout history as being run in its owners' absence by a series of cellar-masters, some good, some idle, some dishonest, producing wine either for the Greiffenclau table, or as gifts and bribes for the political suzerains. In general, the Greiffenclaus served the Prince Bishop Electors of Trier and Mainz, often occupying those offices themselves. Thus in 1370, we read that "Freidrich Greiffenclau von Folraths is representative and Ambassador of Archbishop Gerlach of Mainz at the court of the Holy Roman Emperor, Charles IV, in Prague."

Their most notorious member was the warrior Archbishop, Richard von Greiffenclau who, clad in armour, with a sword at his side, rode off to war. An artillery expert, he invented the most powerful siege-gun of his time; at the siege of Trier in 1519, he went round the fortifications himself checking every defence point, arming his priests and marshalling the nuns into a fire-watching squad. One of the few references to his wine in the archives is in connection with these nuns. They evidently became so unruly that he ordered their transfer to an isolated place lower down the Mosel. When they refused, he "bribed them to go with *ein halb Fuder Wein* (half a cartload of wine)". At the time of the Peasants' War, he ordered all the knights of the land to come to him armed, "in harness and iron helmet", and he led them into battle, at the head of 800 mounted knights and 1,200 infantry. They slaughtered 4,000 of the insurgent peasants, and he executed another 800. Pfister in his *Geschichte der Deutschen* (vol 4.82) says that by this act the Archbishop "smeared the good name of the Greiffenclaus", because "he carried out some of the executions with his own hand."

When the Greiffenclaus were not being military, they became devout; there are as many bishops and monks as firebrands in their family history. One of them in the fourteenth century was so devout that he abandoned wife, family and Schloss Vollrads to set off on a crusade, stopping on the return journey to enter a monastery near Ragusa, where he ended his days. The habit of going into monasteries sometimes endangered the continuity of the line. The Greiffenclau Archbishop of Mainz (1626–1629) considered that as he had two younger brothers, the line was assured; but one of them suddenly joined the Barefoot Order, and the other died without issue. Whereupon the Archbishop and head of the family ordered the Barefoot one to leave his Order and to marry. This he dutifully did, he produced the requisite heir, and the line was saved.

It appears that the Greiffenclaus did not take up permanent residence at Vollrads until the seventeenth century. In 1680, we find Georg Philip von Greiffenclau living there with his two wives (consecutively), and twenty-six children. He was a man of taste, responsible for the Baroque architecture which is still today the principal interior feature. Another who became Prince Bishop of Würzburg (Karl Philip von Greiffenclau, 1749–54) was also artistic, commissioning the famous Tiepolo staircase ceiling in the Residenz.

In 1847, the male line became extinct, and the last member of the long line of Greiffenclaus, Sophie von Greiffenclau, married the Count Matuschka of Silesia. By royal permission, the name of this illustrious family became Matuschka-Greiffenclau. The grandson and present Graf married Eleonora Countess of Neipperg, and they have three sons. Thus once again, the great name of Greiffenclau has been saved from extinction.

The present Graf, Richard von Matuschka-Greiffenclau, lives at Vollrads, where he has devoted his life to viticulture, being one of the greatest experts on the subject in Europe. His book *Neuzeitlicher Weinbau* is a study of the most modern methods for combating grape diseases, including the dreaded phylloxera, which came to Germany later than to the rest of Europe. At a time when hybrid grafting (the Californian graft) was little known in Germany, he induced the Prussian administration to establish a laboratory and testing vineyard at Bad Ems, and a viticultural school at Oranienstein. After the Second World War, in 1949, he had the distinction of leading the first German delegation to an international conference (the viticultural conference in Athens), when Germany was still something of an international outcast. His personal charm and learning on that occasion smoothed the way for German participation at all subsequent international conferences. In 1953, he introduced the revolutionary Lenz-Moser system to the Rheingau, by which the vines are grown higher and further apart. This enables modern machinery to move more easily between them. The method has since been adopted by most leading German vineyards. He was also instrumental in forming the *Deutsche Weinbauverband* to protect vineyard estates. Thanks to men like him and his contemporary peers, such as the Prince Metternich, the German wine industry, hitherto a laggard among its European counterparts, has been brought fully into the twentieth century.

13

Two Great English Houses
Gilbey and Sandeman

The big wine firms so far described concentrate exclusively on one product of the grape. Ricasoli, Ingham, Forrester traded in, respectively, Chianti, Marsala, Port. The same can be said for the Rothschilds in Bordeaux, or the Bollingers and de Vogüé in Champagne. But there is one English firm with multifarious interests in fermented juice, W. & A. Gilbey. Today their business extends to the ends of the earth, where they sell almost every known form of alcohol. In the Médoc, they own the château of Loudenne where they produce their own claret; they have wine stores at Jarnac on the Charente, where they make their own cognac; the same can be said of their wine lodges in Oporto and their production of port; at Mainz on the Rhine, they bottle their own hock and mosel; in Rheims they make champagne, and at Saumur on the Loire, sparkling wine; at Jerez de la Frontera, large *bodegas* store their sherries. Not content with the juice of the grape, they have installed whisky distilleries at Rothes in Moray-shire and Keith in Banffshire, and a gin distillery at Camden Town. We are therefore hardly surprised to see a Gilbey publicity photograph depicting crates of their produce being transported on the backs of shaggy llamas across the Bolivian Alps at a height of 12,000 ft. To what corner of the globe has this egregious firm not penetrated?

Yet diversified as their interests are today, they started humbly enough, with one interest only, and that totally unconnected with wine. The first Gilbey was a stage-coach owner.

By the end of the eighteenth century, the English stage-coach and post was the swiftest and most efficient in Europe – thanks

largely to McAdam's transformation of our roads from a laby-
rinth of ruts and pot-holes into a hard and uniform surface. On
the Great North Road stood four hundred coach-horses, one for
each mile of the journey from London to Edinburgh, The coaches
travelled at ten miles an hour, and persons along the route used
to set their watches when they passed.

Among those who took great pride in his smart and efficient post
service was Henry Gilbey of Bishop's Stortford, proprietor of the
coach operating between that town and London, a distance of
some thirty miles, which he accomplished twice daily. As this
was also part of the road to Cambridge and Newmarket, it brought
him into contact with a variety of passengers, academic and sporting who appreciated his jovial manner and fund of anecdotes. He
generally held the ribbons himself, and sometimes had the honour
of driving the Prince Regent – who showed his appreciation on one
occasion by giving Gilbey one of his own horses.

Henry Gilbey was born in 1789, the year of an ominous pro-
phecy for him, which he was in his life-time to see literally ful-
filled. Even at the end of the eighteenth century, people could still
not envisage any swifter means of transport than by horse on
land and sail by sea – with the exception of Erasmus Darwin
who, in his *Loves of the Plants*, wrote the following prophetic
lines :

> Soon shall thy arm, resistless steam, afar
> Drag the slow barge, and drive the rapid car.

He was right. Within a decade railway lines were beginning to
stretch out all over the country. Soon the well-appointed coaches
with their spanking teams were losing customers. Soon valley, hill,
moor and woodland were resounding to the steam-whistle instead
of to the merry flourish of the post-horn. To Henry Gilbey and
many like him this meant gradual stagnation. He had already
given a number of hostages to fortune, in the shape of six sons
and as many daughters – to whom at his death he appears to have
bequeathed little beyond a good name and his irrepressible energy.
His sons had to make their way in the world, and the two younger
ones – who concern us here – Walter and Alfred Gilbey, started as

clerks in a firm of Parliamentary agents. When the Crimean War broke out in 1854, they gave the first indication of that initiative and drive which was to mark their careers. They volunteered for service as civilians, obtaining employment in the Army Pay Department, and were sent out to the Near East. In those days the Pay Department discharged duties which would, properly, have belonged to the medical staff had there been one (Florence Nightingale had not yet arrived at Scutari). For nearly two years, the Gilbey brothers worked in a hospital at Gallipoli, and had their fill of horrors of that pestilential war. When it ended in 1856, they returned to London where, having lost their Parliamentary work, they had to make a second start in life.

For Walter, now aged twenty-six, and Alfred twenty-two, the prospect was not bright. But acting on the advice of their elder brother, who ran a small wholesale wine business, and with his modest financial assistance, they took cellars at the corner of Berwick Street and Oxford Street, where they started in a small way as retail wine merchants under the name of W. & A. Gilbey. Possessing not a half-crown of capital between them in that year, 1857, their most sanguine hopes can hardly have foreseen what that name would mean by the end of the century.

At this time, the consumption of European wines in Great Britain was confined almost entirely to the rich and well-to-do. The duty of twelve shillings on a dozen bottles of French wine placed them beyond the pocket of most people. On *colonial* wines however, from the South African Cape, the excise duty was only five shillings and sixpence a dozen. The Gilbey brothers decided to take a risk and forsake the traditional French market. They decided to concentrate exclusively on these cheaper colonial wines, obtaining thereby small profit, but catering for a market potentially far bigger than that of French wines. This boldness was rewarded, for within a year they had on their books some 20,000 customers, representing trifling sums individually, but much collectively.

They soon began to look for wider fields than London, and opened up branches for their type of wine in Dublin and Edinburgh. At the same time, they took certain family relations into the firm, thereby following a clannish impulse which, from the outset, has been a distinguishing feature in W. & A. Gilbey. Their eldest sister had married James Blyth of Chelmsford, whose younger son, Henry Arthur, was brought into the firm soon after he left school. He proved to have a remarkable head for figures, and was soon put in charge of the accounts. His appointment was to play a considerable part in their future success, for his regularity and promptness in settling bills gave the firm great prestige in commercial circles. Two of the younger Gilbey sisters had married the Gold brothers, Henry and Charles, who were also taken into the firm.

The rapid extension of the business soon exceeded the capacity of their modest premises, and in 1859 they opened an office at 357 Oxford Street, with cellars under the Princess Theatre. In 1860, they acquired larger premises in Great Titchfield Street, also with new cellars. The administrative part of the business was rearranged, Walter undertaking the office work, while Alfred was put in charge of the cellars and personnel. They had to feel their own way, for they had struck out on a new line, and the wine trade at that time possessed no firm to which they could look for guidance or example; no other firm had adopted the principle of selling wine at a small profit but in large quantities.

At this moment in 1860, after such initial success, they received their first set-back. Cobden's famous trade agreement with Napoleon III caused a fiscal revolution in England. The preference granted to colonial wines was withdrawn, and the duty on French wines reduced from twelve shillings to two shillings a dozen. A death blow to the Cape wines, this threatened to be as fatal to the Gilbeys' budding business as the railway had been to their father's.

Once again they took a calculated risk. They realised that the only course open to them was a dangerous one – but with true instinct, they determined to take it. Observing that the old-established wine firms were taking advantage of the budget provisions by not reducing the price of claret and burgundy to customers to the full extent of the duty exemption, the upstart house of Gilbey, scarcely four years old, announced that it would allow its customers the full benefit from the lowering of the duty. Had these young men hesitated – had they attempted, as they might have done successfully if their firm had been of older standing – to take the profit from the reduced duty, their business would probably not have been heard of again. As it was, this bold line secured them a lead which they were never to lose.

As pioneers in the trade with low-priced wines, and in these adventurous courses, W. & A. Gilbey had to struggle against an immense amount of prejudice. People who had been in the habit of paying high prices for good wines could not believe that the reduction of duty from one shilling to twopence a bottle was not connected with inferior quality. Even today, a century later, many people believe that cheapness is synonymous with inferiority, and are guided in purchasing by price rather than quality. Yet the Gilbeys were introducing an immense amount of sound, palatable wine, such as had never found its way to England since the days of Queen Elizabeth. They made wine what it had not been for centuries – a commercial article instead of a luxury.

The reduction of duty on French wines was not the only feature of Cobden's agreement with France which the Gilbeys turned to good account. Before 1860, the retailing of wines and spirits was restricted by law to hotel-keepers, publicans and wine merchants. The government now permitted the purchase of wine from grocers and holders of "off" licences for consumption at home – on the Victorian theory that the home consumer would suffer less temptation than if he drunk in a public house.

Hitherto, the Gilbeys had dealt directly with customers from their branches in London, Dublin and Edinburgh; but the institution of the "off" licences opened a new field for enterprise. Grocers in provincial towns were quickly enlisted to act as agents, because the Gilbeys realised that by selling through these local agencies, they would not have to pay commercial travellers. The first towns in which grocers were enlisted were Reading, Torquay and Wolverhampton; but from all over the country applications to act as Gilbey agents came pouring in, far more than could be granted immediately. In a few years, most of the Gilbey customers drew their supplies through local agencies rather than from the Oxford Street headquarters.

Gladstone spoke highly of the firm, and in his later years had dealings with it. This caused certain malevolent tongues to spread the rumour that he was in some way interested in it pecuniarily. More than once he denied publicly that he had any connection whatever with Gilbeys. Four years before his death having been recommended by his doctor to drink a certain astringent kind of wine, and having failed to obtain it anywhere, he applied to Messrs Gilbey. They immediately succeeded in procuring the wine for which their services were acknowledged by the Prime Minister in the following letter:

Hawarden. August 27th, 1894

Dear Sirs,

You have indeed outstripped all my requests, and I thank you very much. . . . I may truly say that I have always regarded the proceedings of your firm with peculiar interest. You have been, as far as I am able to form an opinion, in an eminent sense, and in a degree with which no one can compete, the openers of the wine trade. The process has, I trust, been satisfactory to yourselves; it has certainly been one highly beneficial to the country; and (like the great enterprise of Messrs. Cook) you stand outside and above the rank of ordinary commercial houses.

I remain, dear Sirs,
With much respect,
Faithfully yours,
W. E. Gladstone.

Since then the honesty of Messrs. Gilbeys' methods has been revealed in their refusal to adopt the principle of trade secrets. Any special methods which have contributed to their success, they have freely communicated to those who care to learn them. This is revealed in their annual statement in *The Times* on the character and results of the European vintages. At first, people were inclined to look askance on these communications in a newspaper as an indirect form of advertisement by a pushing firm. But the accuracy and abundance of the information obtained from their continental producers, and the frankness with which all features, favourable

131

and unfavourable, were revealed caused this annual letter to be regarded as authoritative.

In the wine trade, as in most commodity businesses, the greatest and most regular profit is obtained by the middleman. The Gilbey partners now decided to become themselves middlemen, between the producer and the consumer. They had seen that the produce of the more remote European vineyards passed through a number of hands before being shipped to England, with corresponding increase in cost to the customer. They decided in 1863 to buy direct from each producer in his own country. Accordingly Alfred Gilbey and James Blyth made their first tour through the wine districts of France, establishing the direct relations with the growers which have continued to the present day. A series of yearly journeys followed, during which every wine-producing country in western and central Europe was visited. Without the intervention of continental agents, the price of Gilbey wines became considerably lower than that of other firms. At the same time, the public became aware that Gilbey's protected them from certain fraudulent methods of blending then practised in France.*

An example of this was seen in the introduction into England by Gilbey's of the sparkling Saumur wine – for the first time under its own name. In 1873, Alfred Gilbey and James Blyth, while visiting the Champagne district, discovered that large quantities of cheap sparkling wine produced on the lower Loire were being shipped to England where it was sold as champagne. As Saumur lies two hundred miles south-west of Epernay, this was clearly fraudulent. Gilbey's therefore arranged for the importation into Britain of the sparkling wine of Saumur under its own name, and its introduction to customers on its own merits, at a price much lower than that of champagne. The result was highly satisfactory; Saumur is now well-known in England, and has a regular if restricted market under its own name.

The reports which the Gilbey representatives wrote of their journeys contain much general as well as technical information – as for instance the one on Spain and its cork-trees. The advantages

---

*Since the imposition of *Appellation controlée* in 1923 these methods have been much restricted.

deriving from direct relations with the wine-growers proved so considerable that Gilbey's entered in Spain into a similar arrangement with the producers of another material essential to the wine trade, cork. This extract is taken from the report by James Blyth and Charles Gold in 1876:

> ... we find that the whole of the province of Gerona is devoted to the growth of cork wood, the mountains being covered with its trees in all directions. It appears a very easy way for men to invest their capital, and peculiarly suited to the Spanish temperament, for very little supervision or outlay is necessary. For example, we heard of one proprietor of a cork forest who sold annually £3,000 worth of cork wood, and his only expense was £60 a year for "stripping" the trees. ... When you hear of the enormous quantities of corks exported annually, it would naturally seem that with its slow growth, the stock would soon be exhausted; but we are told that only one-third of the cork forests of Spain are worked at all, the bulk of this kind of property being in the hands of Spanish noblemen ...

In the eighteen years since its foundation the firm of W. & A. Gilbey had grown to dimensions which should have satisfied most ambitious merchants. Already acting as their own middlemen, and owning "off" licences all over Britain, they found this not enough; they now aspired to becoming their own producers. They decided to buy a vineyard and château in the heart of the claret country, the Médoc. In 1875 they purchased from the Vicomtesse de Marcellus the Château de Loudenne, some forty miles north of Bordeaux, a property covering 500 acres. For this they paid £28,000, which was a big sum in those days. They installed a new *chais*, and a *cuvier* or press-house with workmens' cottages. They entirely reconstructed the farm buildings and added to the château. They built a small harbour on the nearby Gironde, with a tramway from the *chais*.

But at this point when they were barely installed, disaster struck. Until now, the Médoc had not been visited by the terrible scourge, the *Phylloxera vastatrix*, which had come to Europe from North America. Such is the fecundity of this insect that one female dying in March will, by the following October, have produced a progeny of twenty-five million. The insects descend to the roots of the vine whose vitality they sap by sucking the juices. The Gilbeys were put to enormous expense in combating this plague, the only effective method being with the costly sulpho-carbonate of potassium. After several years, by freely soaking the soil with this, and by grafting the Cabernet-Sauvignon grape on American stocks, the pest was finally eliminated.

The Gilbey purchase of Loudenne was much appreciated locally. When they bought the château in 1875 the wage-bill in the vineyards was £516 a year; by the end of the century under their management, it was £6,500 a year. In 1887, Loudenne received from the French Ministry of Agriculture the Gold Medal for the best managed vineyard in the Gironde.

No account of this firm can close without describing its most outstanding member, Sir Walter Gilbey, Baronet, who died in 1910, known outside the trade for his rearing of live-stock. The love of horse-flesh must have been in his blood, derived from the old coaching days at Bishop's Stortford. Agricultural draught-horses were his first concern; and the high standard of shire horses in England today can be traced to the small company he founded in 1877 for the purchase of two Old English cart stallions. Three years later, having paid what appeared at the time the incredible price of 900 guineas for the stallion Spark, he founded his own shire-horse stud at Elsenham. This coincided with the publication of the first volume of his *Shire Stud Book*. The result of his example and labours is apparent to this day in the massive, sweet-eyed animals which have replaced the undersized, underfed work-horses with their ragged quarters and drooping ears which served English farmers throughout the eighteenth and early nineteenth centuries.

From cart-horses, Sir Walter Gilbey extended his attention to other breeds. In 1882, when foreigners were bidding high for the champion Hackney stallion, Danegelt, he determined that such a prize must not leave our shores; he bought the horse from his owner, a publican, for 5,000 guineas. He founded the London Cart Horse Society, with its now famous annual parade on Whit

Monday. In 1893, a baronetcy was conferred on him for these public services; and in 1896 he was further honoured by his appointment as President of the Royal Agricultural Society. In 1900, Queen Victoria appointed Gilbey's Purveyors of Wines and Spirits to Her Majesty.

We have here traced the rise of the modest enterprise founded in 1857 by Walter and Alfred Gilbey, through means of a small loan from their elder brother. The capital now invested in the firm is ten million pounds, and the annual sales amount to twenty million bottles.

One of the features of these nineteenth-century wine firms was the decision of the founder to live abroad among the vineyards, and not to return to his native land until he had made a fortune. Ingham in Sicily said he would not return to Yorkshire until he could buy up the entire district he was born in; by the end of his career he could have done so ten-fold. George Sandeman, founder of another famous firm, said much the same thing. In the Sandeman's archives today is a letter to his sister in their native town of Perth, in which he declares that he will not return there until he has made a fortune. To achieve this, he adds, he will allow himself nine years unless "some fortunate circumstance should reduce the time to six years". Such was the self-confidence of these tough nineteenth-century business men. To help him buy a wine vault, his father lent him £300. In spite of all his self-confidence, he can hardly have imagined that from so modest an origin, his business would in thirty years have expanded to world-wide proportions, with its great wine lodges in Oporto and *bodegas* in Jerez.

At first, George Sandeman carried on the London side of his business at Tom's Coffee-house in Cornhill. This may seem strange today, but it was customary during the eighteenth century for city merchants to transact their business in London's many coffee-houses. (In Lloyd's Coffee-house the famous Insurance Institution was founded in 1770.) He then began a series of travels abroad, chiefly among the vineyards of Spain and Portugal with which his name is so closely associated today. In spite of the Peninsular War, he travelled widely in search of the best and cheapest grapes. On one occasion at Torres Vedras, he dined with the Duke of Wellington and discussed with that wine connoisseur the best port vintages.

At his death, he was succeeded by his nephew, George Glas Sandeman (1792–1868), who extended the business in a number of directions, including insurance and the export of linen and cotton goods to the Americas. But these new undertakings were not detrimental to the wine business which continued to expand and flourish – evidence of this being the firm's purchase of its own clipper, The Hoopoe, which plied between Oporto and the eastern ports of England.

The Sandemans strengthened the Portuguese connection in 1856, when one of them married the eldest daughter of the Portuguese Ambassador to the Court of St James's, the Visconde da Torre de Moncorvo. But the most outstanding member of the family in modern times appears to have been Walter Albert who, after the Great War, when the new American commercial methods were penetrating England, realised that the wine business was too old-fashioned compared with other trades. He introduced high-powered American type advertising. His many reforms included, we have seen, the introduction of the company's now universally known Don figure trade mark. At the time this was considered grossly vulgar by the more conservative firms. The members of the Factory House in Oporto still believed that "a good wine needs no bush"; but they had to admit that it increased Sandeman's sales tenfold.

The head of the firm today is Mr Timothy Sandeman who recently moved the premises from the City to the Albert Embankment. From here he looks out on to a riverside scene as animated as that of the Douro, flowing past the elegant building on the Riva da Gaia which Robert Carr of York built for his ancestors nearly two hundred years ago.

14

The Burgundian Dukes

We have now retreated considerably in time from the nineteenth century, the heyday of the wine personalities. The seventeenth and eighteenth centuries had a lesser crop and, in general, with the receding centuries they become harder to identify. However, the fifteenth century in Burgundy yielded four colourful figures, the Valois dukes, who ruled that province for a hundred years. Aware that wine was their most precious commodity, they earned from the French nation the title of *Seigneurs des meilleurs crus de la Chrétienté*. They owned vineyards at Beaune, Pommard, Volnay, Meursault, Aloxe-Corton, all names which stir the imagination today, whose wine they stored in the vast cellars of the ducal palace at Dijon. In the words of the French historian Courtépée, "They guarded their vineyards as they did their jewels." Such was their power and wealth in that short period of Burgundian greatness, and the magnificence of their court in Dijon, that the court of France itself was eclipsed.

Under their beneficent rule, the Burgundian vineyards were greatly extended; a whole world of artisans lived from their vines, besides the ordinary vineyard workers – coopers, hoop-makers, gaugers, wine-carriers. The greatest of the dukes, Philippe le Hardi, was a good-humoured, swashbuckling, hard-fighting character who could drink any man under the table. He earned the soubriquet "Hardi" (bold) at the battle of Poitiers where, at the age of sixteen, he fought like a lion. We see him today in his famous tomb in the Salle des Gardes at Dijon, lying on his back at peace, the hands crossed piously on the chest, the powerful mouth and prominent fleshy nose, and the cynical smile of a man as accustomed to the exercise of power as to the pleasures of the table.

In 1395 he drew up with his own hand the Edict by which the planting of the Gamay grape was forbidden in his domains. Although this grape yields a larger quantity than the Pinot grape, the wine is much inferior – in the Duke's own words, *"moult nuisible à la créature humaine"*. He wished to set a high standard because, as he wrote, "The wines between Beaune and Dijon can be the best and most precious in the world." As a result of his efforts, he was later able to proclaim proudly, "The highest persons in Christendom now drink my wine. The King of France, the Pope at Avignon and many others give their preference to it, although they could provide themselves more cheaply and abundantly from other sources if they wished."

The Duke Philippe appears to have been the first vineyard owner in history to appreciate the value of publicity. When he was at Bruges with the other Great Powers negotiating peace with England in 1398, he ordered that at all the official banquets and celebrations only his Beaune wine should be drunk. The other negotiators, among them the Black Prince, so appreciated his wine that, after the Treaty was signed, they ordered large consignments of it. Philippe also took his Beaune wine with him when he represented the King of France at the papal palace in Avignon. The cardinals there drunk it freely, too freely it appears, for Petrarch said that one of the reasons why they refused to return to Rome was because that city had no Beaune wine. The ducal palace archives in Dijon are full of references to the despatch of Beaune wine to kings, popes and European dignitaries.

The Duke Philippe was also famed for the immense banquets he gave in the ducal palace. He appears to have been aware, four hundred years before Talleyrand, of the role that wine could play in diplomacy. The word "banquet" derives from his seating arrangements at these feasts – a huge horse-shoe table with benches (*bancs*) around it; the guests sat on these with their backs to the wall (the chair as we know it was not used). He also invented the *escriteau*, (menu) which was circulated at the table to inform the guests of the fare. He gave Charles VII of France such a banquet in Dijon that the monarch had to be assisted from the table after it, and four hours afterwards, "he could emit no sound from his mouth save squeals of joy".

The chronicler Olivier de la Marche has described one of these Petronian feasts in the Ducal Palace:

The Hall was hung with sumptuous tapestries and guarded by archers in gold brocade. In the middle stood a table laden with gold and silver service and crystal vases studded with gold and precious stones. On one of the vast side tables was a monster *pâté* in which 28 living persons were playing musical instruments. On the other side of the table stood an imitation château, its moat filled with vine juice, and crowned by the figure of the fairy Melusina seated on a turret.... In the middle of the meal, a giant entered leading an elephant caparisoned in silk. This was followed by a flying dragon which traversed the room on a pulley....

The food at these entertainments appears to have been equally grotesque: Lark *pâté* with plucked eagle chitterlings, stuffed suck-ing-pig with wild boar preserves, rabbit *à la menthe*, swan's bisque, roast peacock, pullets, elderberry fritters, fennel tart, *crêpe* of medlar. These are only a few of the dishes listed by the mediaeval chronicler, for the English gastronomic dictionary is unable to do justice to the other French delicacies offered on that occasion – *cornils*, *gasttelets*, *ordettes*, *fourmantières*, *cognards*. The historian adds that the Duke Philippe poured out the wine for his guests, taking it with his own hands from the Ganymedes continually bearing flagons to the tables.

Nor did this business-like monarch neglect the commercial opportunities offered at these banquets. He introduced a curious kind of *entremet* between courses, which took the form, not of the usual delicacies but, while the sated guests were digesting the previous course, of Burgundian artists, craftsmen and tradesmen who paraded in front of the tables, displaying their wares. By turns, contemporary Burgundian shoes, costumes, embroidery, jewellery, paintings, sculptures would be placed before the guests. The latter were naturally in an expansive mood, and would buy readily or place orders with the artists for their own or their families' portraits and busts.

Incredible as it sounds, the Duke Philippe died bankrupt. A contemporary chronicler wrote at his death in 1404, "His debts surpassed the immense revenues of his Duchy. Seized by creditors, his furniture was publicly sold. His widow had to raise a loan to pay for his funeral. In spite of her Ducal title, she had to renounce her widow's rights, and to depose, as was the custom in the case of bankruptcy, on the coffin of her deceased spouse her belt, her keys and her bag."

The Valois Dukes were also responsible for the appearance of a very different kind of "Prince of the Grape", their Chancellor, Nicolas Rollin, founder of the Hospices de Beaune, one of the best-known wine establishments in the world. Born at Autun in 1417, of modest origins, his father being a wine-dresser in the service of a nunnery, he quickly revealed a remarkable aptitude for figures when helping his father with the accounts. It was therefore decided that he should enter the law. He passed his exams brilliantly, and came to the notice of Philippe le Bon, Philippe le Hardi's grandson, who took him into his employment as an accounts clerk. His stewardship of the ducal vineyards was so successful that he soon obtained promotion to the closest counsels of the Duke. By 1450, he was Philippe's right-hand man, his Chancellor and Lord Privy Seal.

A hard-faced businessman if ever there was one – as we see in Van Eyck's portrait in the Louvre – Nicolas Rollin, in the course of the next twenty years, promoted not only the ducal fortunes but his own. Quite how he amassed his vast fortune is not known, but references to bribes for contracts are fairly frequent in the Dijon archives, a common enough practice among politicians then, as now. This is endorsed by his decision to build the Hospices in Beaune for the poor, which was prompted by expiatory motives. In his own words in the Act of Donation, "Desiring as I do by Fortunate Commerce to exchange for Celestial Wealth the Temporal Wealth that I owe to Divine Bounty, to exchange the Perishable for the Eternal, I found and endow irrevocably in the city of Beaune an Alms House for the poor and sick, with a chapel in honour of Our Lord and His glorious Mother Mary, Eternal Virgin . . ."

These fine words were not echoed by Louis XI, who heartily disliked Rollin, describing him thus, "It is very right and proper that a man who has made so many poor people suffer should, before he dies, build a palace for those same poor people."

A palace it certainly is, more like a royal residence than a haven for the poor, raising to the skies, as if still imploring God to take pity on the sinful soul of its founder, the clear line of its sharply inclined roof, covered with the famous glazed and brilliantly coloured tiles.

It was not until 1518 that the Hospices began to acquire its vineyards (well after Rollin's death), through donations and bequests from pious or contrite persons on their death-beds. This continued for over four hundred years until, by the Revolution, the Hospices owned more vineyards than any other establishment in France, with *clos* in Pommard, Volnay, Corton. Thus the Hospices became known to the world for a reason which Nicolas Rollin could not have conceived nor approved; for their wine rather than for their charity. When we talk today of *Les Dames Hospitalières* of Beaune, or *Les Dames de la Charité* of Beaune, we are referring not to pious ladies, but to labels on bottles. The founder, too, would be surprised to find himself known to the drinking public by a bottle called *Le Chancelier Rollin*.

15

The Vineyards of the Lord

The figures of the vinous popes and bishops of the Middle Ages are somewhat shadowy, and only one or two have come down to us with any personal detail. The vineyard of Pope Clement V outside Bordeaux still produces the wine known today as *Pape Clément*. He was Bertrand de Goth, Archbishop of Bordeaux, elected Pope Clement V in 1306 and then, as a result of the intrigues of the King of France, transported bodily from Rome to Avignon where he inaugurated the famous "Babylonian captivity" of the popes, which lasted seventy years. He was a man of great wealth, as his many possessions in his native Gascony reveal. Even today, six hundred years later, the famous vineyard from which he entertained his visitors is still regarded as one of the finest in the Graves; it is certainly the oldest *named* vineyard in France. History accuses Clement V of many vices – cupidity, shameful gastronomic excesses and *amours* with the Princesse de Périgord, to whom he gave a *maison de plaisance*, with a vineyard at Pessac. He also possessed the vast unfinished castle of Villaudrant on the slopes of the Ciron. It still stands today erect after six centuries, the ravages of the French Conquest of 1453, and the wars of the Leaguers, who fired some 1,200 cannon-balls into its almost indestructible walls. With its vast ogival windows and Norman arches, it seems to proclaim the existence of a past race of giants.

Standards of conduct then were so different from our own that we find it hard to understand such a man. On the other hand, another Pope, John XXII, who laid out the vineyard known today as *Chateauneuf du Pape*, just above Avignon, comes down to us very clearly in Alphonse Daudet's charming little *conte*, *La*

Mule du Pape. "There was in Avignon," he writes, "a good and aged Pope who loved, above all else in life, the vineyard which he had planted himself six leagues from Avignon among the myrtle groves of Châteauneuf. Every Sunday evening after Vespers, this worthy man would repair on his mule to pay court to his vineyard. Here, seated in the shade of the trees, with his mule tethered beside him, and his Cardinals gathered around him, he would open a flagon of the fine ruby coloured wine called *Châteauneuf du Pape*. He would enjoy it in small sips while gazing tenderly at the vines. Then, the flagon emptied and dusk falling, he would contentedly return on his mule to Avignon, followed by his Chapter."

In the Dark Ages, in a Europe racked by barbarian invasions, civilisation existed only in the abbeys and monasteries. The monks reclaimed the land with their own hands; by intelligent rotation of crops, they gradually restored the abundance and fertility of Roman times. Here, they were inspired by the great Saint Benedict of Subiaco, who enjoined that devotional exercises should be allied with manual labour. He recommended the monks to "build monasteries in localities which provide the necessities of life – water, a mill, a garden, a bakery, a vineyard". The last word is significant.

The monks' farms were model farms, their barns, granges and viticulture the best in Europe. They alone could read the treatises, they alone knew from Virgil that no vine should be placed upon a westward-facing brow (the Georgics: *"neve tibi ad solem vergant vineta cadentem"*). To the superstitious peoples of the first millennium they seemed the confidants of God, alone capable of casting the horoscope of the land. In that "Age of Faith", whenever some natural phenomenon such as a storm, a drought, a flood or an insect intrusion blighted the vines, recourse was had to the Church for an incantation to repair the damage and repel the intruder. A procession would be formed which, headed by the priest chanting litanies, would make its way to the blighted vineyard. Here, after the priest had sprinkled Holy Water on the vine, he would pronounce the following anathema against the noxious animalcule: "I adjure Thee Brother Water by the God above, who at the beginning separated Thee from dry matter, to become a fount of well-being, a shield against the ambuscades of Satan. Thus all weevils, moles, caterpillars and grasshoppers, when Thou fallest on them, shall flee this vineyard."

Such was the superstition in the late tenth century, that all men went in fear of the year 1000, convinced that it would bring with it the end of the world. As that fateful hour approached, work was interrupted, trade languished, the vineyards were neglected – by everyone save the monks. When the year 1000 came and went without the Crack of Doom, a grateful population hastened to build more churches and monasteries.

In that age when the secular rulers, the barons and seigneurs, were often as superstitious as their subjects, they too hastened to ingratiate themselves with the Church. One of the features of the Dark and Middle Ages was the number of vineyards granted as donations to the monasteries by rich seigneurs, frequently on their death-beds. In 1181 Anseric II, Sénéchal of Burgundy, gave the Abbey of Pontigny his vineyard at Chablis, assuring the monks that it possessed a white wine "which will keep a long time" (in those corkless days an unusual virtue). The Order of Malta received from the Seigneur de Sennitier the vines of Aigue and Marsonnets. Often humbler persons contributed in the same way – the old man tormented by the sins of his past; the wife craving indulgence for her husband's return from the wars; the mother soliciting Paradise for her deceased infant. Thus in 1240, "the spouses Gauthier and the widow Fauconnier" donated to the Nuns of Notre-Dame de Tart their vineyard in the Clos de Tart. From AD 560 onward, for over a thousand years, the registers of the churches and monasteries are full of vineyard donations.

In this way, the greatest of all the ecclesiastical vineyards was founded. In 1100, the monks of Cîteaux in the Côte d'Or were granted by Hugues Chevalier de Vergy, a local seigneur touched by remorse or grace, a piece of land between the Beaune-Dijon highway and the chestnut woods covering the lower slopes of the Côte. This precious plot, known today as the Clos de Vougeot, was then little more than waste land, with here and there a few grapes growing wild. The monks of Cîteaux had little experience of viticulture; but within a decade or so they had planted it with vines which were producing one of the best growths on the Côte. As the Abbey of Cîteaux was too far away from Vougeot for daily work (ten kilometres), a modest habitation for the monks who worked the vineyard was built in the Clos, together with a small chapel, cellars and wine-presses. These monks were known as *Frères Convers*, to distinguish them from their fellows, the *Frères de Choeur*, who were occupied exclusively with prayer and meditation. For seven hundred years these *Frères Convers* cultivated the Clos de Vougeot; from generation to generation, these priestly cellarers transmitted as a sacred trust the accumulated fruit of their experience. When at the Revolution in 1789 the Clos de Vougeot was sequestrated, it comprised a hundred and fifty acres of the finest wine grapes in the world.

In the course of these centuries, many more donations were made to Cîteaux, and it became one of the richest monasteries in France. Such was the renown of its wine by the fourteenth century, that Vougeot was being drunk by the papal as well as the ducal courts. In 1371 the Abbot of Cîteaux sent thirty casks of Vougeot to Pope Gregory XI at Avignon. It is significant that His Holiness soon afterwards made him a Cardinal.

In the early days when the monks were devout, they worked in the vineyards contemplating God in His Heaven through the clusters of grapes, glorifying His bounty in allowing them to produce such nectar. But by the sixteenth century a change was beginning to take place – devoutness replaced by jocundity. The popular image of the jovial, *embonpoint* monk seated at the well-garnished refectory table, washing down a haunch of venison with a flagon of good red Burgundy, dates from this time. In the *Physiologie de Goût*, Brillat-Savarin writes of these ecclesiastics' liking for good food and wine. He describes a certain Canon Rolet of Cîteaux who drank so much Burgundy that he became mortally ill. The doctor confined him to bed, and forbade him to touch another drop for the rest of his life. But on visiting the sick cleric some weeks later, the doctor was horrified to find on the patient's beside table a goblet, a napkin and an empty bottle of Burgundy. On reproaching the monk severely for thus courting death, he received the reply from the bed: "Doctor, you will recall that when you forbade me to drink wine, you did not forbid me the pleasure of contemplating an empty bottle. That is what I now do all day long."

Similar tales are told in these later times about the monasteries – that high thinking and low living had been replaced by the pleasures of the table and the bed. In certain monasteries, in order to provide an excuse for drinking, the monks poured libations to every saint and angel they could think of, not only to Christ, His Mother, the Holy Ghost and the Apostles, but to every birth, death and marriage in the parish at which they had to officiate. The abuse became so flagrant that the Archbishop of Rheims strictly forbade, "All libations in honour of any angel or saint, or for the repose of souls."

The transfer of the papal court to Avignon was responsible, at least in part, for this secular transformation of the clerics. Papal documents as early as 1319 refer to the arrival in that year at the papal palace in Avignon of a large consignment of Beaune wine, along the Saône and the Rhône. Twenty years later, the wine of Beaune had become so popular among the Avignon cardinals that they refused to leave Avignon and return to Rome. In a letter to Pope Urban V in 1366, Petrarch beseeches him to transfer the seat of St Peter back to Rome, adding sarcastically, "The Cardinals now cannot live a happy life without the wines of Beaune; to them it is the Fifth Element." Contemporary Provençal sources confirm the affection with which the Beaune wines were held at the papal court. That town, says the author of *Desputosion du Vin et l'lane*, is the Queen of the Vineyards because:

> le pappe l'ama tant
> que beneisson li donna.*

"Beneisson" is the Provençal for "recovery", which may well explain why Innocent VIII in the twelfth year of his Pontificate wrote to the Duke of Burgundy thanking him for a consignment of his wine: "Beloved Son, Greeting! This wine of Beaune which thou hast sent me is of an excellent and agreeable flavour. It is

*The Pope loved it so because it cured him.

particularly suited to Our Nature and complexion. We have employed it regularly during Our last illness."

Another writer about the papal court at Avignon, M. Pierre Andrieu, describes how the communicants were shocked one day when Cardinal de Bernin celebrated Mass in an excellent Beaune. When asked why he did not use the ordinary Communion wine, he replied, "Because I do not want the good Lord to see the wry face I pull whenever I drink that muck." The same author relates that the chaplains of Saint-Martin-de-Tours wished to enlarge the vineyards they owned in the Chablis region by one belonging to a grand seigneur. The price he asked, 2,000 pounds, was more than they possessed, so they sold the gold covering on the great altar of Saint Martin to obtain the money. As M. Andrieu says, "Just as the alchemists of the Middle Ages were able to transmute base metals into gold, so the chaplains of Saint-Martin-de-Tours found a way of turning gold into wine."

In Cognac as late as the eighteenth century, the monks still had their alembic from which they distilled their *eau-de-vie* and sold it. So profitable was this source of income, that the state attempted to levy a tax on all bottles of *eau-de-vie* used for commercial purposes. In 1713 the local archives contain this entry: "The priests inhabiting the Grande Champagne de Cognac met today at Augeac-Champagne to solemnise the feast of the Conversion of St. Paul." It goes on to show, however, that his vision on the Damascus road was not their main preoccupation. They had come together outraged that the fiscal authorities had imposed this annual tax on "the wine which they burn in their cauldrons by *la bonne chauffe* method to convert into *eau-de-vie* to sell to the merchants". The assembled priests all swore "with the hand on the heart" that they had never paid such a tax in the past, and would never pay it in the future. The Abbot of Bourg-Charente declared that throughout his twenty-five years in the diocese he had never "seen nor heard said that any dues could be demanded for *eau-de-vie* from ecclesiastics." The curé of Verrières declared that he had for years been converting "by *la bonne chauffe* the wine of my living into *eau-de-vie* without being taxed."

It was the same in the monasteries. In the archives is a reference to the Benedictine Abbey of Bassac, to "two domestics required in the burning room". Thus when before dawn, the candles were being lit in the chapel, and the Angelus was sounding the hour of mattins, and the chorus of the monks arose, in the "burning-room" of the monastery *la bonne chauffe* was already in progress.

The great wealth which the church had amassed through its vineyards by the eighteenth century is depicted in a caricature from the early French Revolutionary period. Entitled *Le Nouveau Pressoir du Clergé*, it shows a number of well-fed and prosperous looking abbots being placed under their own wine presses, the levers of which are being manipulated by two *Sans-culottes*. From the abbots' fat bellies a hail of gold coins pours out, as their bodies are relentlessly pressed further and further, reducing the great, fat figures seen at the beginning of the pressing to the leanness of church mice.

The Revolution brought the end of the ecclesiastical vineyards. Dispossessed by the Convention their decline, as we have seen, had really begun three centuries earlier. To visit Cîteaux today is a sad experience. Once directors of the greatest vineyard in France, the present monks seem hardly aware of their glorious viticultural past. I asked one of them sitting at the receipt of customs, where he was selling post-cards to tourists, if he had any literature about that past. He looked at me blankly and said, "All we make today at Cîteaux is butter-scotch. It is the best in Burgundy." *Quelle dégringolade!* Their ancient Clos de Vougeot now belongs to some fifty small private proprietors, each of whom produces his own brand of what he calls *"Clos de Vougeot"*. To achieve quick returns, most of these owners employ the inferior, quantity-producing Gamay grape rather than the expensive Pinay which the Dukes of Burgundy had insisted upon in their vineyards.

For the best part of a thousand years the Church had produced the finest wines in Europe. *Vinum theologicum* was held superior to all other wines, for the monks concentrated on quality rather than quantity. The learning of which in the Dark and Middle Ages they were the sole repository, allied with the unique opportunity for research which their retired pursuits allowed them, had made them aware earlier than other men of the best methods for cultivating the growth, and controlling the fermentation, of the grape.

Only at Hautvillers outside Epernay, monument to monkish viticulture still remains, the tomb of Dom Pérignon in the Abbey Church. It is now the property of the firm of Moët et Chandon who maintain it as a shrine for wine-lovers, who come from far and wide to pay their tribute to the greatest of the monkish wine-makers.

16

Ausonius in Bordeaux and Horace in Tivoli

The first tree you should plant on the mellow soil
of Tibur is the vine.

Horace's advice to his friend Varus.

(Odes. I. xxiii)

In spite of its fame as the greatest wine-producing region in the
world, Gascony appears not to have known the grape in the early
days of Roman occupation. Strabo makes no mention of it in his
topographical survey of the Roman empire; nor does Caesar in
De Bello Gallico, when enumerating his commissariat problems.
If wine for his troops had been available, a Roman general would
surely have made some reference to it, for in Rome's long martial
history, the outcome of many battles has been influenced by the
sobriety, or insobriety, of the opposing forces. Caesar's silence
is significant. The inhabitants of Roman *Bordigala* (Bordeaux)
drank beer made from barley, and later were familiar only with
the wine brought to Gaul from Italy.

The explanation appears to be that the Romans inhabiting
Provincia Nostra (what we call Provence today being then
regarded as a part of Italy) wished to retain a monopoly of
Italian wine. The Roman Senate enacted that other transalpine
peoples of the Empire – which included all the Gallic tribes –
should not cultivate the grape or the olive, in order to maintain
the price of, to quote Cicero, "*our* wines and *our* olives". The
local Gallic population was thus denied the considerable commercial advantages which the Roman *negotiatores* derived from the
sale of wine. Although some vineyards were later installed by the
Romans on the Côte d'Or in Burgundy, nearly all the wine drunk
in France came from Italy by boat in *amphorae* to Marseilles,
whence it was despatched into the interior.

A further reason for this relative absence of the grape in France
until the end of the third century was that the Emperor Domitian,

last of the Twelve Caesars, considered that the shortage of wheat, which was becoming acute throughout the Empire, was the result of over-production of wine, which required less effort to cultivate. He therefore forbade all further vine plantation in the Empire, and ordered half the vineyards in Italy to be uprooted. This happened in AD 92. It was not until nearly two centuries later, in AD 286, that the Imperial Edict was revoked by the Emperor Probus, the son of a gardener. The whole Empire, the provinces included, could now cultivate the grape.

This ruling was greeted throughout the Empire, and particularly in Bordigala with the greatest jubilation. The vineyards were planted to the accompaniment of pagan rites and Bacchic ceremonies (Christianity was not yet the official faith). By the fourth century, Bordigala's native Latin poet, Ausonius, was singing the praises of the local oysters and "our glorious wines."

> Ostrea ...
> *Non laudatur minus nostri quam gloria vini**

Gascony had suffered greatly from the invasions and confusions of the third century; but by the time of the poet Ausonius (AD 310–393) all traces of this had vanished, and man had almost forgotten the evil times. In Ausonius's poetry, Gascony is a land of peace and plenty, of vineyards and cornfields and palatial country villas. He was the brilliant child of that Gallic Renaissance in the fourth century, a kind of "Indian Summer" between two periods of barbarian convulsion. Faith in the stability of the Roman Empire again seemed untroubled. There is no hint in his verse of the dim hordes already mustering on the northern frontiers who were, within twenty years of his death, to be established on the banks of the Garonne.

In that civilised fourth century AD, the aristocratic families of Bordigala, to which on his mother's side he belonged, eschewed the calling of arms, (later to be the only one for a nobleman) in favour of the arts and letters. To write good Greek and Latin was considered more important than to wield the sword; and the Academy of Bordigala in the fourth century was the first in

---

*"Oysters, no less praiseworthy than our glorious wines".

Gaul. Its masters were in demand in Rome and Constantinople; Ausonius himself, as tutor to the Imperial family, taught the young Gratian, who was later to assume the purple. Few aristocracies in history have been so civilian and so civilised as that of Bordigala.

It has often been assumed that Roman society at this time, both in the homeland and the provinces, was essentially urban in its tastes and character, that the love of the countryside was introduced much later by the Transalpine races. This was not so in the fourth century, when the safety of the countryside attracted the rich away from the towns to the amenities of their rural villas (the word "amenity" springs from those days: *amoenus*, outside the city walls). Ausonius spent some years in Bordigala teaching rhetoric, but when he had attained wealth and distinction, he could barely endure the life of the city, for even a short visit. He expresses his disgust at the crowds and noises and sordid life of the narrow streets; he longs for his vineyard at Lucanius, just north of the Dordogne, and the spacious freedom of the countryside. His poetry exhales this love for the fresh beauty of rural scenery and the abundance of a great estate. In a letter to his friend, Paulinus, he writes, "Here, separated from Bordigala and its crowded streets, I devote my mind in peace to the vineyard slopes, the rich land which rejoices the farmer's heart, the green meadows, the wood with its shifting shadows."*

In his verse, we feel the scenery of the Garonne, verdant meadows, vineyards on the banks and yellow cornfields rippling under the passing breeze. He refers to "my vineyards reflected in the blond Garonne", and to a passing boatman, "his gaze fixed upon the greenish grape vines". "Life here," he writes in one poem, "is all joyous where the grape vine leaps to embrace the sky, and the grapes turn golden, where the vine-dressers are the envy of the lesser, coarser tradesmen." He frequently describes his vineyards at dusk, when the fields are deserted by humans, and the blue-eyed Naiads have taken possession, together with rustic satyrs and Pan with his cloven hoof. He describes how he once came upon the

*Ep XXVII. 90-94. An excellent description of life in Gascony at this time, is contained in Charles Johnston's *The Last Romans* (in preparation).

beautiful Panope stealing a bunch of his grapes on the slopes, and then flying off to join the Oreades "playing with the lascivious fauns".

In these years of retirement, his vineyards were his chief delight, and he contrasts their richness with those of his neighbours. In that twilight of civilisation when the roads were relatively safe, there was much visiting between country friends. The tedium of running an estate could be relieved by passing on to a neighbour's, or by receiving his visit in return. Travelling by road or river in those days in Gascony was probably easier and quicker than it was for an English squire in the eighteenth century. Couriers passed to and fro bearing friends' letters, trifling presents and lines of verse, maxims and apophthegms. Although Christianity had become the official faith, this was still essentially a Pagan society in its tone and habits, concerned more with ethics than morals, satisfying its appetites as if unconscious that it had any, expending its intellectual energy on the Greek and Latin classics of the past.

Ausonius refers to the Roman villas on the banks of the Garonne almost as if they were Hadrian's at Tivoli – the parks, thermal baths, libraries, statues, picture galleries. Jocundity is the principal element of his verse connected with the grape, and the quality he praises most is "infatuation" with the joys of drinking. *Laetus* and *joca* are the words which recur most often in his poems. In Epistolae XV he writes, "Let us find in the cup a sweet relief for the sadness of the soul ... for all around us are the gifts of Ceres, fecund in earthly fruit ... there, mix as you see fit the nectar of the grapes." Like another writer, Montesquieu, fourteen centuries later, Ausonius often said he was prouder of his vineyard than his poetry. This may well be so, for his verse is often uneven. Mr Cyril Connolly describes Ausonius a "a voluble poet who has since been underrated because he produced too much bad work".*

Within twenty years of Ausonius's death, the barbarian hordes had descended from the north, and the night of the Dark Ages came down. The towns, hitherto open, became so many fortresses; the stately Roman country villas became *châteaux-forts*; and the heirs of a civilised aristocracy took to the profession of arms.

*In The *Sunday Times*, 24th December, 1972.

Yet just before that decline, when the twilight of the Roman world still seemed full of hope and colour, this native poet evoked the echoes of another, a greater Latin poet, at the other end of the history of the Roman Empire, Quintus Horatius Flaccus:

> Goblets were made for jollity; only Gauls
>   Use them to fight with. Gentlemen, behave!
> For Bacchus has a character to save,
> And not participate in murderous brawls.
>
> Daggers are out of place among good wine
>   And lighted candles. Stop that wicked noise,
>   And keep your elbows on the cushions, boys!
> We didn't meet to quarrel, but to dine.

So sang Horace four centuries before Ausonius, in one of his drinking Odes to the guests who had come out from Rome to dine at his Sabine Farm. Horace knew what a "Gaul" was, from Caesar's *De Bello Gallico* and, like Ausonius, but with more reason, he found it inconceivable that these boors should ever have dominion over Roman territory. Indeed these two poets, at the opposite ends of the Empire, had much in common: both gentle satirists of public life and morals, both lovers of civilised tranquillity and ease, both wine-bibbers and wine-growers. Like Ausonius, too, Horace loved to retire to Nature, on his farm in the Sabine hills some twenty miles north-east of Rome, from the noise and bustle of the capital, there to drink his own wine in the company of friends. In his verse we see him as the thoughtful host, seated before his hearth, plying the guests with food and drink. Many of his Odes take the form of invitations to these friends, tempting them to come out from Rome and share the pleasures of his table:

> Now Comrades, to drink deep,
> Now with the free foot to beat the ground,
> Now with rich feasts and goblets crowned
> The tables of the Gods to heap!
> Bottle on bottle in swift relay
> And dance and song the whole night long.

His small farm lay in the valley of the Licenza, not far from

Tibur (the modern Tivoli), and its remains can still be visited today. A few miles north of Tivoli, the valley widens into a kind of natural amphitheatre, where you leave the road and, directed by sign-posts to the *Villa di Orazio Flacco*, ascend a ridge through a grove of olives, to emerge on the far side in full view of the farm laid out below. Considering that 2,000 years have passed, it is in a state of remarkable preservation. The basement walls of about twenty symmetrically placed rooms clearly demarcate the buildings as they must have been in Horace's day. There was a rectangular patio to the south enclosing the vineyard, and two other courtyards with covered porticoes which offered shade to the stroller in the heat of a Roman summer; a Nymphaeum with fountains; and a small swimming-pool.

In his dislike of the capital, Horace is the Latin poet who most clearly saw the fault of his age – the mania to grow rich rather than happy and wise, to sacrifice the true ends of life to the pursuits of material gain. In his Odes and Epistles he satirises this, repeatedly telling us that "the wise man cannot be happier than when drinking wine drawn from the grapes around the trellis work above his table." Certainly, he had on this farm all that a Greek philosopher could desire – a comfortable if modest hearth under an everlasting sun, fanned by the breezes of the south, a goat, a few kids, some sheep and fowls – and the vineyard. In the warm spring evenings, he says, the song of the cicadas came up from the olive groves, and innumerable fireflies twinkled in the dusk. We can imagine him taking what he calls his "Sunset walk" along the mountainside, looking out across the Campagna to the Alban Hills and, on the horizon twenty miles away, the great *Urbs* itself.

On that semi-tropical hillside beside the farm grew, together with the *pizzutello* grape from which he made his wine, strawberries, peaches, pears, apples and cherries – a cornucopia of fruit. It is hardly surprising that in this countryside, so rich with flora too, the local chroniclers should claim that it was here, in this Sabine vale, not in Sicily, that Persephone collecting hyacinths with her maidens was surprised and spirited away by Pluto to the infernal regions – whence he allowed her to return to Earth but once a year, bringing with her the phenomenon of Spring. Horace's garden was well-stocked, he says, with flowers and statues, and near the villa sparkled the waters of a spring, "fresher and purer than those of the Thracian Hebrus". Listening to this water in a myrtle wood dedicated to Faunus, Horace used to quaff beakers of Falernian wine:

> Plain myrtle, boy, a spray for each will deck
> Beseemingly both you who fill the cup
> And me who drain it lying
> Under the woven vine.
> (Odes I. xxxviii)

Bibliography

A *short selection*

Andrieu, Pierre *Petite Histoire de la Bourgogne et de sa Vignoble*
  (Montpellier 1955). Also similar accounts by the same author
  of Champagne and Bordeaux.
Bradford, Sarah *The Englishman's Wine* (Macmillan 1969)
Caraman-Chimay, Princesse Jean de *Madame Veuve Clicquot-
  Ponsardin – sa vie, son temps* (Debar, Rheims 1956)
Delaman, Robert *Histoire de Cognac* (Jarnac 1967)
Dion, Roger *Histoire de la vigne et du vin en France des
  origines au 19 siècle* (Paris 1959)
Forbes, Patrick *Champagne, the Wine, the Land, the People*
  (Gollancz 1967)
Hancock, W. K. *Ricasoli and the Risorgimento in Tuscany*
  (Fertig. New York 1969)
Jeff, Julian *Sherry* (Faber 1961)
Penning-Rowsell, Edmund *The Wine of Bordeaux* (Michael
  Joseph 1969)
Ray, Cyril *Cognac* (Peter Davies 1973)
Ray, Cyril *Fide et Fortitude* (the House of Barton) (Pergamon 1971)
Ray, Cyril *Lafite* (Peter Davies 1968)
Ritter, H. *Deutscher Wein Bilder aus der Heimat und der
  Geschichte des deutschen Weins* (Trier 1907)
Russell, Mark (ed) *The Paragon of Wines and Spirits*,
  Vol. 2 (Heidelberg Publishers 1972)
Trevelyan, Raleigh *Princes under the Volcano* (Macmillan 1972)
Vogüé, Bertrand de *Madame Veuve Clicquot et la conquête
  pacifique de la Russie* (Paris 1960)

Index